Veggie chic

hamlyn

Veggie chic

Rose Elliot

First published in Great Britain in 2006 by
Hamlyn, a division of Octopus Publishing Group Ltd
2–4 Heron Quays, London E14 4JP

ISBN-13: 978-0-600-61399-2
ISBN-10: 0-600-61399-2

A CIP catalogue record for this book is available from the British Library

Printed and bound in China

10 9 8 7 6 5 4 3 2 1

Buy cheese with the vegetarian symbol to ensure it is made with vegetarian rennet and buy vegetarian Parmesan-style cheese instead of traditional Parmesan which is not vegetarian. Always check the labels of preprepared ingredients to make sure they do not contain non-vegetarian ingredients such as gelatine.

Vegetarian Society APPROVED

Notes

Both metric and imperial measurements are given for the recipes. Use one set of measures only, not a mixture of both.

Ovens should be preheated to the specified temperature. If using a fan-assisted oven, follow the manufacturer's instructions for adjusting the temperature. This usually means reducing the temperature by 20°C (65°F). Grills should also be preheated.

Free-range medium eggs should be used unless otherwise specified. The Department of Health advises that eggs should not be consumed raw. This book contains some dishes made with raw or lightly cooked eggs. It is prudent for more vulnerable people, such as pregnant and nursing mothers, invalids, the elderly, babies and young children, to avoid uncooked or lightly cooked dishes made with eggs.

Vegan recipes are labelled 

Fresh herbs should be used unless otherwise stated. If unavailable use dried herbs as an alternative but halve the quantities stated.

This book includes dishes made with nuts and nut derivatives. It is advisable for those with known allergic reactions to nuts and nut derivatives and those who may be potentially vulnerable to these allergies, such as pregnant and nursing mothers, invalids, the elderly, babies and children, to avoid dishes made with nuts and nut oils. It is also prudent to check the labels of preprepared ingredients for the possible inclusion of nut derivatives.

Salt and pepper: use sea salt and freshly ground black pepper, unless otherwise specified.

contents

introduction

When I was asked to write this book I was thrilled. I've been wanting to write a 'decadent' vegetarian cookbook for some time, to show just how luxurious and delectable the food can be, and to address the perennial question 'what can I do for vegetarian entertaining?', and here was my chance. But veggie *chic*? What exactly did that mean?

The dictionary was consulted: 'elegant and stylishly fashionable; graceful', it said; 'pleasingly ingenious and simple'. A picture was emerging: recipes that were a bit different – fresh, bold, stunning yet simple. They also had to be easily achievable, because to me 'chic' also implies confidence, ease and effortlessness. And definitely have a bit of the 'wow factor'. When I've spent time and energy cooking a special meal, one of the joys, apart from the taste of the food and the pleasure of the company, are the 'oohs' and 'ahs' that greet the dishes – and the empty plates at the end of the meal. What cook doesn't love that?

I set about inventing, testing and tasting what I hoped were 'pleasantly ingenious and simple' dishes. I had a lot of fun creating these and many memorable meals. Some were simple. There was the evening when I made the Mixed Mushroom Tempura and we all sat around the kitchen table, glasses of wine in hand, trying the crispy golden morsels, hot and crunchy, straight out of the pan, with various dips to see which went best. Well, that was the excuse...

Different, but equally successful, was the party when I wanted to try out as many of the recipes as I could. The Baby Yorkshire Puddings with Nut Roast and Horseradish were the undisputed stars of that party and deserve special mention. They definitely passed the 'wow factor' test, but in fact everything in that section of the book – Party time – passed the 'not a crumb left' test.

Another unforgettable occasion was the summer feast when we had the Bloody Mary Jellies followed by Salad of Warm Artichokes and Chanterelles, then the Individual Pea, Spinach and Mint Pithiviers, with a final flourish provided by the Pink Champagne Granita Marbled with Raspberries. That menu may sound a bit daunting, yet when you analyse it, each of the four courses is actually quite simple and a lot of the preparation can be done in advance – one of the keys to successful and stress-free entertaining.

When I was working on this book I tested the

recipes on whoever happened to be around. People tried them, gave me their opinion and recipes were changed and adapted accordingly. So the recipes don't belong to some special 'chic' group: they have general appeal and can be made by anyone with average kitchen skills.

They can also be adapted to suit the occasion. For instance, you'll find that the majority of the recipes have a simplicity about them and also allow for advance preparation. The Rice Noodles with Chilli-Ginger Vegetables, for instance, the Squash Stuffed with Moroccan Rice, the Bubble-and-Squeak Cakes with Beetroot Relish, the Portobello Steaks en Croûte – these, and others like them, are easy to do. You can serve them just with a salad or a vegetable accompaniment, or you can build them into a fantastic menu of several courses, if you wish.

Alternatively, go for drama with a stunning centrepiece such as the Chickpea Flatcake Topped with Lemon- and Honey-Roasted Vegetables, the Potato and White Truffle Torte, or the Dauphinoise Roulade with Red Chard and Dolcelatte Filling. There are so many possibilities; how simple or showy, relaxed or formal you make the feast is up to you.

My advice is this: whatever you are cooking and for whatever occasion, whether it's rustling up a quick meal for one or two after work, or preparing a five-course dinner for ten, cook what you love to eat. If you're entertaining, get organized as much as you can in advance – and if you're nervous, or want to spend the maximum time with your guests, choose dishes that can mostly be made ahead. Then – and this is most important – relax and have fun!

Remember, there's so much more to food than just ingredients and recipes. It's also about pleasure, generosity, warmth and sharing, not whether you've got everything absolutely restaurant-perfect (you eat out for that). It's the spirit behind it that counts, that's what makes food healing, soothing, bonding, cheering, uplifting and nourishing for the soul as well as for the body, and what will make your food special. Giving others pleasure through the food you cook must be one of the simplest yet most profound joys there is.

Rose Elliot

sumptuous starters and side dishes

The perfect starter awakens and tantalizes
the taste buds ready for the delights of
the main course – and is easy to make,
with most of the preparation done in advance.
These recipes fit the bill and there are also
some delectable side dishes which really
complement the main course.

hot pomegranate and pecan leafy salad

serves 4
preparation 10 minutes
cooking 12 minutes

100 g (3½ oz) pecan nuts, roughly broken
1 tablespoon balsamic vinegar
2 tablespoons olive oil
250 g (8 oz) peppery leaves, such as rocket or watercress
1 pomegranate
salt and pepper, to taste

1 Spread the pecan nuts out on a baking sheet and place in a preheated oven, 180°C (350°F), Gas Mark 4, for about 12 minutes, or until lightly browned and aromatic. Remove from the oven and tip on to a plate to prevent them from burning.

2 Mix the balsamic vinegar, olive oil and some salt and pepper in a large salad bowl to make a dressing.

3 Put the leaves on top of the dressing, but don't toss them. Halve the pomegranate as you would a grapefruit and turn the skin inside out to make the seeds pop out. Add the seeds to the leaves, along with the pecans.

4 Toss the salad and serve immediately.

wakame, cucumber and spring onion salad with rice vinegar

serves 4
preparation 10 minutes, plus soaking

5 g (¼ oz) wakame seaweed
½ cucumber, peeled and shredded
6 spring onions, chopped
1 tablespoon rice vinegar
1 tablespoon mirin (or a dash of honey for non-vegans)
1 tablespoon shoyu or tamari
salt, pepper and sugar, to taste
a few toasted sesame seeds

1 Put the wakame into a bowl, cover with boiling water and leave to soak for 10 minutes, then drain and chop or snip.

2 Put the cucumber and spring onions into a bowl. Add the wakame, rice vinegar, mirin or honey and the shoyu or tamari, mix gently and season with salt, pepper and sugar.

3 Put the salad into a shallow dish or on to individual plates and scatter with a few toasted sesame seeds. Serve at once.

stilton and cherry salad with cinnamon dressing

serves 4
preparation 10 minutes, plus marinating

- 50 g (2 oz) dried cherries
- 2 tablespoons sherry, port or other fortified wine
- 1 large lettuce, torn, or about 450 g (14½ oz) mixed salad leaves
- 50 g (2 oz) blue Stilton, crumbled
- 50 g (2 oz) flaked almonds, toasted

for the cinnamon dressing

- 4 tablespoons olive oil
- 2 tablespoons raspberry vinegar
- 2 teaspoons caster sugar
- 1 teaspoon ground cinnamon
- Tabasco, salt and pepper, to taste

1 Put the dried cherries into a small container, cover with the sherry or port and set aside to plump up – if you can leave them for a few hours, so much the better.

2 To make the dressing, whisk together the olive oil, raspberry vinegar, sugar, cinnamon and several drops of Tabasco – enough to give it a good kick – and some salt and pepper.

3 Put the lettuce or salad leaves into a bowl with the Stilton, almonds and cherries, together with any of their liquid that remains. Drizzle over the cinnamon dressing and toss gently. Serve at once.

I adapted this salad from one served by Chef Robert Bruce in New Orleans. It has a very warming, festive feel.

salad of warm artichokes and chanterelles

butter garlic chives

serves 4
preparation 30 minutes
cooking 50 minutes

4 globe artichokes, stems removed
2 tablespoons olive oil
25 g (1 oz) butter
250 g (8 oz) chanterelle mushrooms
4 garlic cloves, finely chopped
squeeze of lemon juice
1 red oak-leaf lettuce
chopped chives
salt and pepper, to taste

for the vinaigrette dressing
2 tablespoons balsamic vinegar
6 tablespoons extra virgin olive oil

1 Cover the artichokes in boiling water and cook for about 45 minutes, or until a leaf will pull off easily. Drain and rinse under cold water to cool quickly. Pull off the leaves until you get to the central fluffy 'choke', then pull this off gently with your fingers under a cold running tap and discard. Slice the bases thickly and set aside.

2 To prepare the dressing, put the balsamic vinegar, olive oil and a generous seasoning of salt in a lidded jar and shake until combined.

3 Just before you want to serve the salad, heat the olive oil and butter in a frying pan and add the chanterelles and garlic. Cook for a few minutes until they are tender and any liquid has been reabsorbed. Add the sliced artichoke bases and cook for 1–2 minutes to heat them through, stirring often. Season well with a squeeze of lemon juice and some salt and pepper.

4 While the mushrooms are cooking, arrange some oak-leaf lettuce leaves on 4 plates and drizzle with the dressing. Spoon the chanterelle and artichoke mixture on top and scatter with chopped chives. Serve at once.

Provided you have a couple of large saucepans, I think it's easier to cook the artichokes whole and then remove the leaves and choke, rather than trimming them first.

salsify fritters with caper cream

lemon crème fraîche

serves 4
preparation 30 minutes
cooking 20 minutes

700 g (1 lb 7 oz) salsify or scorzonera
2 tablespoons freshly squeezed lemon juice
1 tablespoon olive oil
1 tablespoon red wine vinegar
2 large eggs, beaten
flour for coating
75 g (3 oz) dried breadcrumbs
rapeseed or groundnut oil for deep-frying
salt and pepper, to taste
lemon wedges, to serve

for the caper cream
2 tablespoons mayonnaise
2 tablespoons crème fraîche
1 tablespoon capers, rinsed

1 Wearing gloves to protect your hands (the juice can stain), peel the salsify or scorzonera under a cold running tap, cut it into about 3 cm (1¼ inch) lengths and put in a saucepan of water containing 1 tablespoon of the lemon juice. Don't worry if you can't remove all the skin – some tiny flecks don't matter.

2 Boil the pieces in the water for about 10 minutes, or until tender, then drain and add the remaining lemon juice, the olive oil, red wine vinegar and some salt and pepper. Leave to cool.

3 Meanwhile, make the caper cream. Mix the mayonnaise with the crème fraîche and capers and season with salt and pepper.

4 Dip each piece of salsify or scorzonera into the beaten egg, then into flour, then into the egg again and finally into the breadcrumbs, to coat all over.

5 Heat the oil to 180–190°C (350–375°F), or until a cube of bread browns in 30 seconds, and deep-fry the coated pieces for about 3 minutes, or until they are crisp and golden brown. Drain on kitchen paper and serve at once, garnished with lemon wedges and accompanied by the caper cream.

Salsify is a long, slim root with a dark skin and creamy white flesh within, and scorzorena is similar. If you can't find either of these, you could use canned salsify. Either way, the texture and flavour are delicate and delicious.

hot and sour mushroom soup

lime coriander ginger

serves 4
preparation 10 minutes, plus standing
cooking 15–20 minutes

1 teaspoon vegetarian Thai red curry paste
125 g (4 oz) shiitake mushrooms, thinly sliced
1 small cluster enoki mushrooms, base trimmed off
1 red chilli, deseeded and cut into rings
20 g (¾ oz) packet fresh coriander, chopped
juice of 1 lime
2–3 tablespoons shoyu or tamari
salt, to taste

for the Thai-flavoured stock
2–3 lemon grass stalks, crushed with a rolling pin
6 kaffir lime leaves, plus 6 more to garnish (optional)
stems from a small bunch of fresh coriander
2 thumb-sized pieces of fresh root ginger, peeled and sliced
1 litre (1¾ pints) water

1 To make the stock, put the lemon grass, lime leaves, coriander stems and ginger into a saucepan with the water. Bring to the boil, then reduce the heat and simmer for 10 minutes. Remove from the heat, cover the pan and allow to stand for 30 minutes or longer for the flavours to infuse, then drain the liquid into another pan and discard the flavourings.

2 Add the curry paste, mushrooms and red chilli to the stock, then reheat and simmer for 3–4 minutes, to cook the mushrooms and chilli.

3 Stir in the chopped coriander, lime juice, shoyu or tamari and some salt, then reheat gently. Serve in individual bowls and garnish with a lime leaf, if liked.

This glamorous soup has a long list of ingredients but is incredibly quick to make! Use a medium-sized, long chilli for this – not the tiny, very hot bird's eye type. Make sure the curry paste is vegetarian – read the label.

creamy fennel soup with gremolata

fennel parsley cream

serves 4
preparation 15 minutes
cooking 20 minutes

2 large fennel bulbs, trimmed and sliced
1 onion, roughly chopped
900 ml (1½ pints) vegetable stock
6 tablespoons double cream
salt and pepper, to taste

for the gremolata
2 tablespoons chopped parsley
thinly pared or finely grated rind of ½ lemon
1 garlic clove, finely chopped

1 Gently simmer the fennel and onion in the stock for 15–20 minutes, until very tender.

2 To make the gremolata, mix all the ingredients in a bowl and set aside.

3 Liquidize the fennel, onion and stock in a food processor or using a stick blender, and for an ultra-smooth result pass the soup through a sieve.

4 Add the cream to the soup and season with salt and pepper, then ladle the soup into warmed bowls and top each with a spoonful of gremolata to serve.

butternut squash and orange soup with nutmeg

squash garlic orange

V

serves 4
preparation 15 minutes
cooking 35 minutes

1 butternut squash, halved and deseeded
2 onions, chopped
2 tablespoons olive oil
2 garlic cloves, chopped
juice and grated rind of 1 orange
¼ teaspoon ground nutmeg
900 ml (1½ pints) water
salt and pepper, to taste
chopped parsley, to garnish

1 Put the squash, cut-side down, on a lightly oiled baking sheet and bake in a preheated oven, 200°C (400°F), Gas Mark 6, for 30 minutes, or until tender.

2 Meanwhile, cook the onions in the olive oil in a covered pan over a gentle heat for about 10 minutes, until tender. Stir in the garlic and cook for a further 1–2 minutes.

3 Scoop out the flesh from the butternut squash halves and mix with the onions and garlic, orange juice and rind, nutmeg and some salt and pepper. Purée using a stick blender or food processor, adding a little of the water if necessary.

4 Tip the mixture into a saucepan with enough of the water to make a creamy consistency and heat gently.

5 Serve garnished with chopped parsley.

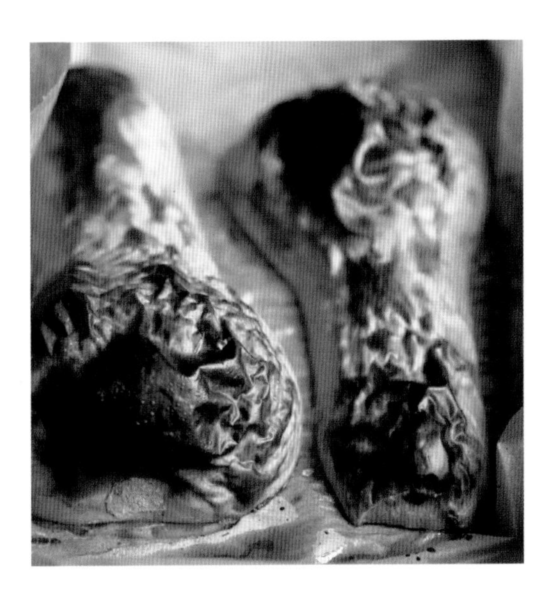

chilled melon soup with mint granita

lemon mint melon

serves 4
preparation 20 minutes, plus chilling and freezing
cooking 5 minutes

1 ripe ogen melon
caster sugar, to taste

for the mint granita
125 g (4 oz) caster sugar
large bunch of mint
300 ml (½ pint) water
1 tablespoon freshly squeezed lemon juice

1 Remove the skin and seeds from the melon and cut the flesh into chunks. Purée in a food processor until very smooth. Taste and add a little sugar if necessary, then chill.

2 To make the granita, put the sugar, mint and water into a saucepan and heat gently until the sugar has dissolved, then bring to the boil. Remove from the heat, cover and leave until cold.

3 Once cold, remove the mint and squeeze it to extract all the liquid. Save about a dozen leaves and discard the rest. Purée the liquid with the reserved leaves and add the lemon juice. Pour into a suitable container and freeze until firm. Remove from the freezer 20–30 minutes before serving, to allow the granita to soften a little.

4 To serve, ladle the melon soup into chilled bowls. Beat the frozen mint mixture with a fork (or whiz chunks briefly in a food processor) and add a scoop to each bowl. Serve at once.

rosemary sorbet

wine rosemary lemon

serves 4
preparation 15 minutes, plus cooling and freezing
cooking 2 minutes

450 ml (¾ pint) water
150 g (5 oz) caster sugar
5 sprigs of rosemary
250 ml (8 fl oz) white wine
4 tablespoons freshly squeezed lemon juice
a few small sprigs and flowers of rosemary, to decorate (optional)

1 Put the water and sugar into a saucepan with 4 sprigs of rosemary and bring to the boil. Remove from the heat, cover and set aside to cool and infuse the flavour of the rosemary.

2 Remove the rosemary from the cooled syrup and stir in the wine and lemon juice. Chop the remaining sprig of rosemary and stir in.

3 Pour the mixture into a shallow container and freeze for about 2 hours, or until firm, scraping down the sides and whisking as it solidifies. Alternatively, freeze in an ice-cream maker until the mixture is soft and slushy, then transfer to a plastic container and freeze until required.

4 Remove the sorbet from the freezer about 15 minutes before you want to serve it, then scoop it into bowls and decorate with rosemary sprigs and flowers, if liked.

Serve as a light starter or as a palate refresher between courses. Be warned – it's quite alcoholic.

aubergine and mozzarella scallops

cheese tomatoes onion

serves 4
preparation 20 minutes
cooking 30 minutes

1 fat aubergine, stem trimmed
olive oil, for brushing
75 g (3 oz) mozzarella cheese
1 egg, beaten
dried breadcrumbs for coating
rapeseed or groundnut oil for deep-frying
salt and pepper, to taste

for the tomato sauce
1 onion, chopped
1 tablespoon olive oil
2 garlic cloves, finely chopped
400 g (13 oz) can chopped tomatoes

1 First make the tomato sauce. Fry the onion in the olive oil with a lid on the pan for about 8 minutes, until almost tender. Add the garlic and cook for a further 2 minutes, then stir in the tomatoes and cook, uncovered, for about 20 minutes, or until very thick. Purée in a food processor or blender, then season and set aside.

2 For the scallops, cut 20 rounds from the aubergine, making them as thin as you can – about 2.5 mm (⅛ inch) if possible. Brush them on both sides with olive oil and cook under a hot grill for about 5 minutes, or until tender but not browned. Season them with salt and pepper.

3 Cut the mozzarella into 20 cubes, put one cube in the centre of an aubergine disc and fold the aubergine over like a mini Cornish pasty to make a 'scallop'. Dip in beaten egg and dried breadcrumbs. Repeat with the remaining aubergine. Put the coated aubergine scallops on a piece of nonstick paper and chill until required.

4 Heat the oil to 180–190°C (350–375°F), or until a cube of bread browns in 30 seconds, and deep-fry the aubergine scallops until crisp and golden all over, turning them as necessary. Drain on kitchen paper.

5 Serve 5 on each plate, with the tomato sauce drizzled around the edge.

Morsels of mozzarella wrapped in thin aubergine slices, crumbed and deep-fried, make a tasty starter, served with tomato sauce.

spinach custards with avocado

nutmeg spinach eggs

serves 4
preparation 20 minutes
cooking 35–40 minutes

butter, for greasing
225 g (7½ oz) spinach
300 ml (½ pint) double cream
2 eggs
1 large ripe avocado
grated nutmeg, salt and pepper, to taste

for the lemon vinaigrette
3 tablespoons freshly squeezed lemon juice
9 tablespoons olive oil

1 Grease 4 x 125–150 ml (4–5 fl oz) ramekins, cups, individual pudding basins or other suitable moulds with butter and line the base of each with a circle of nonstick paper.

2 Wash the spinach, then place in a saucepan with just the water clinging to it and cook for about 6 minutes, or until very tender. Drain well in a sieve, squeezing out as much water as possible, then chop.

3 Put the spinach into a food processor with the cream and eggs and whiz to a purée, then season with grated nutmeg, salt and pepper.

4 Pour the mixture into the greased moulds, stand these in a roasting tin and pour boiling water around them. Bake in a preheated oven, 180°C (350°F), Gas Mark 4, for 30 minutes, or until firm on top and a skewer inserted into the centre comes out clean. Remove from the oven and leave to cool.

5 To make the vinaigrette, whisk the lemon juice with the olive oil and some salt and pepper.

6 Slip a knife around the edges of the moulds to loosen, then turn them out on to individual plates. Peel and slice the avocado and arrange some slices on each plate. Season with salt and pepper, then spoon the lemon vinaigrette over the avocado and the custards and serve warm or cold.

hot hazelnut-coated vignotte with redcurrant relish

serves 4
preparation 10 minutes
cooking 5 minutes

2 x 150 g (5 oz) Vignotte cheese
100 g (3½ oz) skinned hazelnuts, chopped
1 egg, beaten
salad leaves and vinaigrette dressing (see page 15)

for the redcurrant relish
100 g (3½ oz) redcurrants
1 tablespoon caster sugar
squeeze of lemon juice

1 Remove any labels stuck on the cheeses, then cut them widthways into 4 rounds, retaining the rind. Spread the hazelnuts out on a plate.

2 Dip the rounds of cheese first in the beaten egg then into the hazelnuts, making sure that all surfaces are thickly coated. Put the pieces of coated cheese on a sheet of nonstick paper and chill until required.

3 To make the relish, heat the redcurrants with the sugar and lemon juice. Bring to the boil, then remove from the heat and set aside.

4 Just before you want to serve the meal, transfer the cheese to a baking sheet and cook, rind side down, under a hot grill for about 5 minutes, or until the nuts are crisp and golden brown. Gently reheat the redcurrant relish.

5 While the cheese is cooking, line 4 plates with a few salad leaves and drizzle them with a little of the vinaigrette.

6 Serve the sizzling pieces of cheese on top of the leaves, with some of the redcurrant relish spooned on top and the rest in a small bowl.

bloody mary jellies

vodka tomato celery

serves 4
preparation 15 minutes, plus setting
cooking 2 minutes

400 ml (14 fl oz) tomato juice
1 teaspoon vegetarian gelatine (Vege-Gel, see page 185)
1½ tablespoons freshly squeezed lemon juice
6 tablespoons vodka
2 teaspoons vegetarian Worcester sauce (see page 185)
½ teaspoon Tabasco
2 tablespoons each finely chopped red onion, celery and green pepper, plus a little more chopped red onion and celery, to garnish
1 tablespoon horseradish sauce
3 tablespoons single cream
salt and pepper, to taste

1 Put the tomato juice into a saucepan, gradually scatter the gelatine over the cold juice and stir until it has dissolved. Slowly bring to the boil, then remove from the heat immediately and stir in the lemon juice, vodka, Worcester sauce, Tabasco and some salt and pepper.

2 Divide the chopped vegetables between 4 small bowls or glasses. Pour the tomato jelly on top and leave to set for at least 30 minutes. Cool until required but don't refrigerate.

3 To serve, mix the horseradish sauce with the cream and swirl some over the top of each jelly. Scatter a little chopped red onion and celery over each one to garnish.

These jellies are best made not too far in advance and kept in a cool place rather than in the refrigerator. This recipe can be vegan if you use non-dairy horseradish sauce and soya cream from a healthfood shop.

tomato and parmesan tarts with basil cream

pastry basil tomato

serves 4
preparation 15 minutes, plus standing for the basil cream, if possible
cooking 35 minutes

375 g (12 oz) frozen ready-rolled all-butter puff pastry (see page 184)
40 g (1½ oz) grated Parmesan-style cheese
450 g (14½ oz) cherry tomatoes, halved
2 teaspoons caster sugar
salt and pepper, to taste

for the basil cream
bunch of basil, stems removed, leaves lightly chopped
6 tablespoons single cream or olive oil

1 To make the basil cream, mix the basil with the cream or olive oil, season with a little salt and pepper and set aside – this gets better and better as it stands, so can be made some hours in advance if convenient.

2 Spread the pastry out on a board and cut into circles to fit 4 x 10 cm (4 inch) diameter shallow flan tins with removable bases.

3 Put the pastry into the flan tins and trim the edges as necessary. Prick the pastry all over with a fork. Bake in a preheated oven, 200°C (400°F), Gas Mark 6, for 15 minutes until golden brown – the pastry will puff up, so press it down gently with the back of a spoon. Remove the flan cases from the oven.

4 Sprinkle the Parmesan over the top of the flans – this keeps the pastry dry and crisp. Toss the tomatoes with the sugar and some salt and pepper and divide them between the flan cases – fill them generously as the tomatoes will shrink a bit as they cook.

5 Put the flans back into the oven and bake for 20 minutes. Remove the flans from their tins, place on warmed plates and swirl some of the basil cream over the top of each one. Serve at once.

crisp tofu with tomato and lemon grass sambal

chilli garlic peanuts

serves 4
preparation 15 minutes
cooking 15–30 minutes

2 x 250 g (8 oz) blocks firm tofu, drained and cut into cubes
plain flour for dusting
rapeseed or groundnut oil for deep-frying

for the tomato sambal
1 tablespoon olive oil
1 lemon grass stalk, trimmed and finely chopped
1 red chilli, sliced (deseeded if you like)
1 garlic clove, crushed
1 tablespoon soft brown or palm sugar
4 tomatoes, roughly chopped
small handful of fresh coriander, chopped
2 tablespoons ketjap manis or soy sauce
1 tablespoon prepared tamarind (from a jar)
4 tablespoons water
2 tablespoons crushed peanuts, to garnish

1 To make the sambal, heat the olive oil in a saucepan and fry the lemon grass, chilli and garlic for 1 minute. Remove from the heat and add all the remaining ingredients except the peanuts.

2 Toss the pieces of tofu in the flour. Pour enough oil into a wok or saucepan to cover the tofu and heat to 180–190°C (350–375°F), or until a cube of bread browns in 30 seconds. Add the tofu and fry until crisp and golden – this may take as long as 10 minutes – make sure it gets nice and crisp (do it in 2 batches if necessary). Drain on kitchen paper. Serve with the sambal spooned over and sprinkled with the crushed peanuts.

Deep-frying tofu makes it savoury and crisp without being at all oily. Topped with a sweet and sour sambal, it makes an excellent first course or a light main course for 2 people.

sesame-roasted asparagus with wasabi vinaigrette

wasabi sesame oil

serves 4
preparation 10 minutes
cooking 15–20 minutes

500 g (1 lb) asparagus, trimmed
2 tablespoons toasted sesame oil
salt

for the wasabi vinaigrette
1 packet (2 teaspoons) wasabi powder
2 tablespoons warm water
1 tablespoon rice vinegar
1 tablespoon flavourless vegetable oil such as grapeseed
2 tablespoons toasted sesame oil
salt and pepper, to taste

1 Toss the asparagus in the sesame oil, spread out on a baking sheet and sprinkle with salt. Roast in a preheated oven, 220°C (425°F), Gas Mark 7, for about 15 minutes, or until just tender and lightly browned in places.

2 To make the vinaigrette, put the wasabi into a lidded jar, add the warm water and mix to a paste. Add the rice vinegar, vegetable oil, sesame oil and some salt and pepper, put the lid on and shake vigorously for a few seconds until smooth.

3 Arrange the asparagus on individual plates and drizzle the vinaigrette on top. Serve hot, warm or cold.

If you can make the dressing in advance – 24 hours is not too long – the flavour of the wasabi mellows and is delicious and refreshing with the asparagus.

polenta chip stack with dipping sauces

lime avocado chilli

serves 4
preparation 15 minutes–1 hour, depending on the type of polenta
cooking 30 minutes–1¼ hours, depending on the polenta

500 g (1 lb) pack ready-made polenta
or
175 g (6 oz) instant or traditional polenta
1 litre (1¾ pints) water
1 teaspoon salt
rapeseed or groundnut oil for deep- or shallow-frying

for the dipping sauces
4 heaped tablespoons mayonnaise
1 tablespoon sun-dried tomato paste
225 g (7½ oz) jar chunky salsa
1 large ripe avocado
3 tablespoons chopped fresh coriander
juice of 1 lime
pinch of chilli powder
salt and pepper, to taste

1 If using ready-made polenta, blot with kitchen paper, then cut the polenta into chunky chips – a 500 g (1 lb) block will make 24.

2 Or, if using instant polenta, make as directed on the packet. For traditional polenta, heat the water and salt in a large saucepan. When the water comes to the boil, sprinkle the polenta over the surface, stirring all the time to prevent lumps. If you do get some lumps, whiz them away with a stick blender or whisk. Leave the mixture to simmer for 45 minutes, or until very thick, stirring from time to time.

3 Line an 18 x 28 cm (7 x 11 inch) Swiss roll tin with nonstick baking paper. Pour the polenta into the tin, spreading it to the edges and into the corners. Leave to cool and firm up.

4 Meanwhile, prepare the dipping sauces. Mix the mayonnaise with the tomato paste and put into a small bowl. Put the salsa into another bowl. Remove the stone and skin from the avocado and mash the flesh with the coriander, lime juice, chilli powder and some salt and pepper to make a creamy, slightly chunky consistency. Put into a bowl.

5 Cut the firm polenta into chips about 15 cm (6 inches) long and 1 cm (½ inch) wide. Pour enough oil into a frying pan to cover the polenta chips and heat to 180–190°C (350–375°F), or until a cube of bread browns in 30 seconds, then shallow- or deep-fry them. It's easy to keep them separate if you shallow-fry them, but make sure they're submerged in oil and cook them until they are really crisp and golden on one side, then turn them over and cook the other side thoroughly. Drain on kitchen paper. If you get them very crisp, the first batch will stay crisp while you cook the rest – keep them warm on kitchen paper in a cool oven.

6 Pile the polenta chips into a stack on a serving dish – or on individual plates – and serve with the 3 dipping sauces.

You can make these chips using ready-made polenta, which makes them very quick and easy, or you can make the polenta from scratch.

spicy thai noodles

ginger soy coriander

serves 4
preparation 15 minutes
cooking 20 minutes

250 g (8 oz) transparent (cellophane) noodles
2 tablespoons toasted sesame oil
2 teaspoons vegetarian Thai red curry paste
6 spring onions, finely sliced
walnut-sized piece of fresh root ginger, peeled and cut into thin shreds
2 garlic cloves, crushed
2–3 tablespoons rice vinegar
1–2 tablespoons shoyu or tamari
2 tablespoons chopped fresh coriander
salt and pepper, to taste

1 Put the noodles into a bowl, cover with boiling water and leave to stand for 5 minutes, then drain and toss in 1 tablespoon of the sesame oil to prevent the noodles from sticking together. Or follow the directions on the packet.

2 Meanwhile, heat the rest of the sesame oil in a large saucepan, add the curry paste and let it sizzle for a few seconds. Add the spring onions, ginger and garlic and stir-fry for 1–2 minutes, to cook lightly.

3 Add the noodles to the pan and remove from the heat. Add the rice vinegar, shoyu or tamari and some salt and pepper and toss lightly. Stir in the chopped coriander and serve.

Cellophane noodles make a light and tasty accompaniment. If you can't get them, you could use other long, thin noodles for this recipe.

nut and miso pâté with cranberry relish and dill

tofu dill cashews

serves 4
preparation 20 minutes, plus soaking
cooking 15 minutes

75 g (3 oz) cashew nuts
125 g (4 oz) firm tofu, drained
1 garlic clove, crushed
4 teaspoons red miso
1 tablespoon nutritional yeast (see page 184) or a little yeast extract, to taste
1 teaspoon shoyu or tamari
4 teaspoons freshly squeezed lemon juice
white pepper
3 tablespoons chopped dill
4 sprigs of dill, to serve

for the cranberry relish
50 g (2 oz) dried cranberries
150 ml (¼ pint) full-bodied red wine
1 teaspoon olive oil
¼ teaspoon white mustard seeds
1 tablespoon finely chopped onion
1 garlic clove, finely chopped
1 teaspoon grated fresh root ginger
pinch of chilli powder
1 tablespoon caster sugar
1 tablespoon red wine vinegar
salt, to taste

1 First make the cranberry relish. Put the cranberries into a bowl, cover with the wine and set aside. Heat the olive oil in a small saucepan, add the mustard seeds, stir for a few seconds until they start to 'pop', then add the onion, garlic, ginger and chilli powder. Cook over a gentle heat for about 5 minutes, or until the onion is tender.

2 Add the cranberries and their liquid to the pan, along with the sugar, red wine vinegar and some salt. Bring to the boil, then reduce the heat and simmer, uncovered, for a few minutes, until the liquid has reduced and is syrupy and the cranberries are tender. Cool. (This will keep, covered, in the refrigerator for up to 2 weeks.)

3 For the pâté, cover the cashew nuts with cold water and leave to soak for 4–8 hours. Drain. Put into a food processor with the tofu, garlic, miso, yeast, shoyu or tamari, lemon juice and a good pinch of white pepper and whiz to a very creamy pâté. Scrape into a bowl, cover and set aside until required.

4 To serve, stir the chopped dill and 4 tablespoons of the cranberry relish into the pâté. Arrange a spoonful in the centre of each of 4 plates and garnish with a sprig of dill. Serve at once – the pâté loses its bright, fresh colour if left to stand.

This wonderful and unusual pâté was inspired by a recipe that appeared in the *Vegetarian Times*. Serve with strips of warm pitta bread.

braised whole baby carrots and fennel

fennel carrots parsley

V

serves 4
preparation 15 minutes
cooking 30 minutes

2 bunches (about 750 g/1½ lb) baby carrots
400 g (13 oz) baby fennel
4 tablespoons olive oil
4 garlic cloves, sliced
300 ml (½ pint) water
freshly squeezed lemon juice
salt and pepper, to taste
chopped parsley, to serve

1 If the carrots are really young, just scrub them; if they're older, peel them, but in either case keep them whole and leave 1 cm (½ inch) or so of the green stems attached at the top. If the fennel is really young and tender, just trim the tops.

2 Put the carrots and fennel into a saucepan with the olive oil, garlic, water, lemon juice and some salt and pepper and bring to the boil. Reduce the heat, cover the pan and cook gently for about 30 minutes, checking occasionally to make sure they're not sticking. They're done when they feel very tender to the point of a knife, and the water has reduced to a syrupy golden glaze. Scatter with chopped parsley to serve.

These vegetables melt in your mouth and their golden liquid supplies a natural sauce for the dish. They are also very forgiving: they should be really tender, so it's almost impossible to overcook them, and they can be cooked in advance and gently reheated later if this is most convenient. If there are any left over, they also taste very good cold.

parsnips in sage butter

serves 4
preparation 10 minutes
cooking 15 minutes

500 g (1 lb) baby parsnips
25 g (1 oz) butter
1 tablespoon chopped sage
salt and pepper, to taste

1 Cut the parsnips lengthways into quarters, to give long slim pieces. Put them into a saucepan with cold water to cover and bring to the boil, then reduce the heat and simmer for 10–15 minutes, or until tender.

2 Blend the butter with the sage and set aside.

3 Drain the parsnips and put into a warm serving dish, or return them to the saucepan. Season with salt and pepper, then add the sage butter and serve.

A simple yet wonderful combination of flavours.

cabbage with sesame and ginger

V

serves 4
preparation 5 minutes
cooking 5 minutes

1 sweetheart or similar cabbage, shredded
1 tablespoon toasted sesame oil
1 tablespoon grated fresh root ginger
1 garlic clove, crushed
salt and pepper, to taste

1 Heat 2.5 cm (1 inch) of water in a saucepan, add the cabbage, cover with a lid and cook for about 5 minutes, or until the cabbage is tender. Drain.

2 Add the sesame oil, ginger and garlic to the cabbage and stir well. Season with salt and pepper and serve at once.

This very simple treatment transforms cabbage. It goes particularly well with Asian-style dishes.

saffron and garlic mash

cream parsley saffron

serves 4
preparation 15 minutes, plus steeping
cooking 20 minutes

1.1 kg (2¼ lb) potatoes, peeled and cut into even-sized pieces
150 ml (¼ pint) single cream
good pinch of saffron threads
50 g (2 oz) butter
4 garlic cloves, crushed
salt and pepper, to taste

for the garnish
4 garlic cloves
1 tablespoon olive oil
1 tablespoon chopped parsley

1 Cover the potato pieces in boiling water and cook for about 20 minutes, or until tender.

2 Meanwhile, put the cream into a small saucepan with the saffron and bring almost to the boil, then remove from the heat, cover and leave to steep.

3 To prepare the garnish, cut the garlic cloves into thin slices. Heat the olive oil in a small pan, add the garlic and fry for a minute or so until the garlic is golden. Remove from the heat and set aside.

4 Drain the potatoes, reserving the water, then mash with the butter, crushed garlic and saffron-infused cream (no need to remove the saffron threads) to make a smooth, creamy consistency. Add a small quantity of the reserved cooking water if needed. Season with salt and pepper.

5 Spoon the potato into a warmed serving dish, top with the fried pieces of garlic and the oil and some chopped parsley, and serve.

roast potatoes in sea salt and balsamic vinegar

vinegar salt potatoe

V

serves 4
preparation 15 minutes
cooking 45 minutes

1 kg (2 lb) potatoes, peeled and cut into 1 cm (½ inch) chunks
rapeseed or groundnut oil for roasting
salt
balsamic vinegar

1 Put the potatoes into a saucepan, cover with water and bring to the boil, then reduce the heat and simmer for 7 minutes.

2 Pour 5 mm (¼ inch) of oil into a roasting tin large enough to hold the potatoes in a single layer, and put into a preheated oven, 200°C (400°F), Gas Mark 6, until smoking hot.

3 Drain the potatoes and put them back into the saucepan, then put the lid on the pan and shake to roughen the outsides and make them cook more crisply.

4 Tip the potatoes into the hot oil and turn them with a large spoon so that the oil covers them all over. Roast for about 35 minutes, or until the potatoes are golden and crisp, turning them over when the undersides are done.

5 Using a draining spoon, transfer the potatoes to a warm serving dish. Sprinkle generously with salt, drizzle with balsamic vinegar and serve.

Having tried various different oils for roasting potatoes, I've found that rapeseed or groundnut oil give the crispiest results.

dinners to dazzle

Vegetarian main courses often baffle people, so here are nearly enough to have a different one every day for four weeks. Some are simple, some more complex, some are in individual portions, others are big, dramatic centrepieces; all, I hope, have a bit of the 'wow' factor.

red pepper, ricotta and fennel tortellini with tarragon sauce

fennel cheese wine

serves 4
preparation 45 minutes, plus resting
cooking 30 minutes

for the pasta dough
350 g (11½ oz) strong plain white flour, preferably '00'
pinch of salt
3 eggs
1 tablespoon olive oil

for the filling
1 fennel bulb, trimmed
1 large red pepper, halved, cored and deseeded
1 garlic clove, crushed
125 g (4 oz) ricotta cheese
75 g (3 oz) freshly grated Parmesan-style cheese
salt and pepper, to taste

for the tarragon sauce
100 ml (3½ fl oz) vegetable stock (use the fennel water)
100 ml (3½ fl oz) dry white wine
450 ml (¾ pint) double cream
2 good leafy sprigs of tarragon, chopped

1 To make the pasta dough, put the flour, salt, eggs and olive oil into a food processor and whiz until combined. Gradually add enough cold water to make a soft, malleable dough – maybe 4–6 tablespoons. Remove from the food processor and knead on a lightly floured board for a few minutes until smooth, glossy and pliable, then put into a polythene bag and leave to rest for 1 hour.

2 Meanwhile, make the filling. Run a potato peeler down the outside of the fennel to remove any potentially stringy bits. Quarter the fennel and cook in boiling water until tender – 8–10 minutes. Strain – the water makes wonderful stock so save it for the sauce.

3 Grill the red pepper, cut-side down, under a hot grill for about 10 minutes, or until black and blistered in places. Cool, then strip off the skin.

4 Chop the cooked fennel and red pepper finely. Add the garlic, ricotta and Parmesan and season with salt and pepper. Divide into 20 equal portions.

5 To make the tortellini, divide the pasta dough into 20 equal portions. Take one portion and roll out on a floured board, making it as thin as you can – big enough to cut out 2 circles with a 6 cm (2½ inch) cutter. Continue with the rest of the dough, then take 2 of the circles and put a portion of filling in the centre of one. Brush the edges with cold water and place the second circle on top, pressing down the edges well. Set aside and repeat the process with the rest of the circles and filling.

6 Bring a large saucepan of water to the boil. Drop in the tortellini and cook for about 6 minutes, or until the pasta is tender.

7 Meanwhile, to make the tarragon sauce, put the stock, wine and cream into a saucepan and boil until reduced by half and slightly thickened. Remove from the heat, season and add the tarragon.

8 Drain the pasta gently in a colander, then tip it on to a warmed dish, pour over the tarragon sauce and serve.

tagliatelle with leek and morel cream and crisp garlic

leeks garlic pasta

serves 4
preparation 20 minutes
cooking 30 minutes

400 g (13 oz) dried tagliatelle
2 tablespoons olive oil
4 large garlic cloves, cut into thin slices, to serve

for the cream sauce
25 g (1 oz) butter
1 tablespoon olive oil
200 g (7 oz) morel mushrooms, roughly chopped
2 garlic cloves, crushed
600 ml (1 pint) cream – single, double or a mixture
250 g (8 oz) leeks, finely sliced
2 tablespoons chopped parsley
salt and pepper, to taste

1 To make the sauce, heat the butter and olive oil in a pan. Add the morels and crushed garlic and cook gently for 5–10 minutes, until any liquid they produce has boiled away. Pour in the cream and simmer, uncovered, until reduced by half.

2 Cook the leeks in boiling water to cover for 3–4 minutes, then drain (the water makes tasty stock) in a sieve and rinse under the cold tap to preserve the colour. Drain well, then add to the cream mixture along with the parsley and some salt and pepper.

3 Bring a large saucepan of water to the boil, add the pasta and cook for 8–10 minutes, or as directed on the packet. Drain into a colander and return to the hot saucepan with 1 tablespoon of the olive oil.

4 While the pasta is cooking, heat the remaining olive oil in a small frying pan, add the sliced garlic and fry for a few seconds until golden and crisp – be careful not to let it burn and become bitter. Set aside.

5 Add the leek and morel sauce to the pasta in the pan and serve on warmed dishes, or serve the pasta first, then spoon the sauce on top. Either way, scatter with the garlic crisps and serve immediately.

rice noodles
with chilli-ginger vegetables

noodles chillies soy

serves 4
preparation 30 minutes
cooking 20 minutes

for the noodles
200 g (7 oz) rice noodles
1 tablespoon toasted sesame oil

for the sauce
1 tablespoon cornflour
2 tablespoons shoyu or tamari
1 tablespoon caster sugar
1 tablespoon toasted sesame oil
1 tablespoon mirin or dry sherry

for the chilli-ginger vegetables
2 tablespoons flavourless oil, such as groundnut, rapeseed or grapeseed
2 tablespoons finely grated fresh root ginger
4 garlic cloves, crushed
1–2 large mild red chillies, deseeded and finely sliced
1 head Chinese leaves or 4 pak choy, sliced
300 g (10 oz) beansprouts
bunch of spring onions, chopped
150 g (5 oz) mangetout, halved lengthways
1 red pepper, thinly sliced
250 g (8 oz) can water chestnuts, drained and rinsed
bunch of fresh coriander, chopped

1 Bring a large saucepan of water to the boil, drop in the rice noodles and cook for about 4 minutes, or as directed on the packet, until al dente. Drain in a colander, then toss with the tablespoon of toasted sesame oil and set aside until required.

2 For the sauce, stir all the ingredients together and set aside.

3 Meanwhile, prepare the vegetables. Heat a large wok over a high flame until very hot. Add the oil, then throw in thc ginger, garlic and chillies. Let them sizzle, then add all the remaining ingredients except the coriander and stir-fry over the heat for about 10 minutes, until all the vegetables are tender.

4 When the vegetables are tender, give the sauce a quick stir and pour into the pan, then stir for 1–2 minutes until the sauce has thickened and is coating the vegetables lightly. Season with salt.

4 Serve the noodles on a warm serving plate. Spoon the vegetables on top in a big, dramatic heap and scatter with the chopped coriander. Serve at once.

You can do most of the preparation for this dish in advance and finish cooking and assembling it just before serving.

tea-smoked chestnut risotto

rice wine parmesan

serves 4
preparation 20 minutes, plus smoking
cooking 35–40 minutes

for the tea-smoked chestnuts

100 g (3½ oz) uncooked rice
50 g (2 oz) dark muscovado sugar
25 g (1 oz) black tea leaves
1 tablespoon whole allspice
2 tablespoons black treacle or molasses
1 cinnamon stick
2 x 200 g (7 oz) vacuum packs whole peeled chestnuts

for the risotto

1 litre (1¾ pints) vegetable stock
1 tablespoon olive oil
2 onions, finely chopped
2 celery sticks, very finely chopped
2 garlic cloves, finely chopped
400 g (13 oz) risotto rice
100 ml (3½ fl oz) dry white wine
50 g (2 oz) butter
100 g (3½ oz) freshly grated Parmesan-style cheese
salt and pepper, to taste

1 Smoke the chestnuts an hour or so in advance. Line a wok with foil, then put in all the ingredients except the chestnuts and stir gently.

2 Arrange a rack over the wok and place the chestnuts on top. Cover with foil and cook over a medium heat for 10 minutes, then remove from the heat and leave to stand, covered, for another 10 minutes.

3 Meanwhile, make the risotto. Heat the stock, then reduce the heat and keep it hot over a very gentle heat.

4 Heat the olive oil in a large saucepan, add the onions and celery and stir, then cover and cook gently for 7–8 minutes, until tender but not browned. Stir in the garlic and cook for a further minute or so.

5 Add the rice to the pan and stir over a gentle heat for 2–3 minutes, then pour in the wine and stir all the time as it bubbles away.

6 When the wine has disappeared, add a ladleful of the hot stock. Stir over a low-to-medium heat until the rice has absorbed the stock, then add another ladleful, and continue in this way until you've used up all the stock, the rice is tender and the consistency creamy – about 15–20 minutes.

7 Stir in the butter, chestnuts and half the Parmesan, season with salt and pepper and serve, scattered with the rest of the cheese.

gateau of curried rice

cumin spinach onions

V

serves 4
preparation 1 hour
cooking 1 hour

for the rice
350 g (11½ oz) white basmati rice
1 teaspoon turmeric
900 ml (1½ pints) water
2 tablespoons freshly squeezed lemon juice
salt and pepper, to taste

for the vegetable layers
3 onions, chopped
1 tablespoon olive oil
1 tablespoon grated fresh root ginger
4 garlic cloves, chopped
1 tablespoon cumin seeds
1 tablespoon ground coriander
2 teaspoons turmeric
1 small cauliflower, divided into small florets
150 ml (¼ pint) water
20 g (¾ oz) packet fresh coriander
300 g (10 oz) potatoes, peeled and cut into 1 cm (½ inch) dice
250 g (8 oz) spinach
400 g (13 oz) can chopped tomatoes
½ teaspoon dried red chilli flakes

1 Put the rice into a saucepan with the turmeric and water. Bring to the boil, then reduce the heat, cover the pan and cook very gently for 15 minutes, or until all the liquid has been absorbed. Remove from the heat and leave, still covered, for 5 minutes. Then add the lemon juice and stir gently with a fork – this will brighten the colour of the rice. Season and set aside.

2 Fry the onions in the olive oil in a large saucepan for about 7 minutes, then stir in the ginger, garlic, cumin seeds, ground coriander and turmeric and cook for a further 2–3 minutes. Divide this mixture equally between 3 saucepans, to make the 3 fillings.

3 For the cauliflower filling, add the cauliflower to one of the saucepans and pour in the water. Bring to the boil, then reduce the heat, cover the pan and cook gently for about 10 minutes, or until the cauliflower is very tender and the water has disappeared. (Increase the heat and boil it off if it hasn't all gone.) Save some of the fresh coriander to garnish, chop the rest and add to the pan, then season with salt and pepper.

4 For the potato and spinach layer, add the potatoes to another of the saucepans. Cover and cook over a low heat for 10–15 minutes, until the potato is almost tender, adding a very little water if the mixture sticks. Add the spinach, cover and cook for about 10 minutes, or until the spinach is tender. Again, increase the heat and boil for 1–2 minutes if the spinach has produced a lot of liquid. Season.

5 For the tomato layer, add the tomatoes and chilli flakes to the third saucepan and boil, uncovered, for 20–25 minutes, or until very thick. Season.

6 Line a 20 cm (8 inch) deep cake tin with nonstick paper to cover the base and sides. Put a quarter of the rice into the tin and spoon the cauliflower mixture on top, followed by another quarter of the rice, then the tomato mixture, more rice, the potato and spinach, and a final layer of rice. Press down firmly, cover with foil and cook in a preheated oven, 180°C (350°F), Gas Mark 4, for about 20 minutes, or until heated through.

7 Turn out on to a warmed serving platter, strip off the paper, top with a sprig of coriander and serve.

squash stuffed with moroccan rice

serves 4
preparation 20 minutes
cooking 30 minutes

2 small squash
1 garlic clove, crushed
olive oil for greasing
salt, to taste

for the rice filling
175 g (6 oz) white basmati rice
25 g (1 oz) raisins
15 g (½ oz) butter
1½ teaspoons ras el hanout (see page 184)
½ teaspoon turmeric
2 tablespoons lemon juice
8 green queen olives, stones removed, chopped
20 g (¾ oz) packet fresh coriander, chopped

1 Cut the squash in half through their stems. Scoop out the seeds, then rub the cut surfaces of the squash with garlic and salt. Place cut-side down on a well-oiled baking sheet and bake in a preheated oven, 200°C (400°F), Gas Mark 6, for 30 minutes, or until the squash can easily be pierced with the point of a knife.

2 Meanwhile, make the rice filling. Bring half a saucepan of water to the boil, add the rice and bring back to the boil, then reduce the heat and simmer, uncovered, for 8–10 minutes, or until the rice is tender but still has some resistance.

3 Plump the raisins by soaking them in boiling water for 2–3 minutes.

4 Drain the rice. Reserve a couple of tablespoons for decoration. Return the rest to the pan with the butter, ras el hanout, turmeric and lemon juice and mix well. Drain the raisins and add to the rice, along with the chopped olives and coriander. Taste and season with salt.

5 Turn the squash so that they are cavity-side uppermost, then fill the cavities with the rice mixture, heaping it up. Serve immediately, or cover with foil and keep warm in the oven for a few minutes before serving.

Mini squash can be used, but they need to be large enough to be baked in halves and then stuffed, because that way they cook really well.

celeriac rosti with green beans in almond butter

almonds beans oil

serves 4
preparation 30 minutes
cooking 20 minutes

1 celeriac, about 800 g (1 lb 10 oz), peeled and grated
100 g (3½ oz) flaked almonds
2–4 tablespoons olive oil
salt and pepper, to taste

for the beans
250 g (8 oz) slim green beans, lightly trimmed and cut in half
4 teaspoons roasted almond butter (see page 184)

1 Mix the celeriac with the almonds and some salt and pepper.

2 Heat 2 tablespoons of the olive oil in a frying pan large enough to hold 4 x 20 cm (8 inch) metal chef's rings – or you may need to use 2 frying pans. Place the rings in the frying pan or pans and fill with the celeriac mixture, dividing it evenly between them and pressing down well. Cover with a plate or lid and cook over a gentle heat for about 10 minutes, or until the underside is golden brown.

3 Using a fish slice, flip each rosti over (still in its ring) and press down the mixture so that it is touching the surface of the frying pan. Cover as before and cook the second side.

4 Bring 2.5 cm (1 inch) of water to the boil in a saucepan, add the green beans and cook for 3–4 minutes, or until just tender. Drain, return to the pan and toss with the almond butter and some salt and pepper.

5 Place a celeriac rosti on each plate and top with green beans. Slip off the rings and serve.

chickpea flatcake topped with lemon- and honey-roasted vegetables

cumin honey lemon

serves 4–6
preparation 30 minutes
cooking 45 minutes

4 tablespoons olive oil
3 large onions, finely chopped
3 large garlic cloves, crushed
2 teaspoons cumin seeds
3 x 400 g (13 oz) cans chickpeas, drained and rinsed
salt and pepper, to taste
lemon wedges and sprig of flat leaf parsley, to garnish

for the roasted vegetables
900 g (1 lb 13 oz) Jerusalem artichokes, peeled and cut into 2.5 cm (1 inch) chunks
450 g (14½ oz) carrots, scraped and cut into batons
3 tablespoons olive oil
3 tablespoons clear honey
3 tablespoons freshly squeezed lemon juice
grated rind of 1 lemon

1 Start with the roasted vegetables. Put the artichokes and carrots into a roasting dish with the olive oil, honey, lemon juice and rind and some salt and pepper and mix gently. Then roast in a preheated oven, 180°C (350°F), Gas Mark 4, for about 45 minutes, turning the vegetables occasionally.

2 Next, make the flatcake. Heat 2 tablespoons of the olive oil in a saucepan, add the onions and cover and fry gently for 10 minutes. Add the garlic and cumin seeds and cook for a further 2–3 minutes. Remove from the heat and add the chickpeas and some salt and pepper. Mash the mixture thoroughly.

3 Put the mixture into a lightly oiled 30 cm (12 inch) round loose-based flan tin and smooth the top. Cover with foil and bake for 15 minutes, then remove the foil, pour the remaining olive oil over the top and bake for a further 5–10 minutes, until golden – but don't let it get dry. Remove from the oven. Turn the flatcake out of the tin and slide it on to a warm serving dish. Spoon the roasted vegetables on top, garnish with lemon wedges and a sprig of flat leaf parsley and serve.

dauphinoise roulade with red chard and dolcelatte filling

cheese potatoes chard

serves 4
preparation 40 minutes
cooking 45 minutes

for the roulade

olive oil for greasing and brushing
900 g (1 lb 13 oz) potatoes, peeled and thinly sliced
1 garlic clove, crushed
salt and pepper, to taste
green salad, to serve

for the filling

450 g (14½ oz) red chard, leaves and stems separated
175 g (6 oz) dolcelatte cheese

1 Line a 22 x 32 cm (8½ x 12½ inch) Swiss roll tin with nonstick paper and brush with olive oil. Mix the potatoes with the garlic and some salt and pepper, arrange them carefully and evenly in the tin and brush with olive oil. Cover with a piece of nonstick paper and bake in a preheated oven, 200°C (400°F), Gas Mark 6, for 30 minutes, then remove the paper and bake for a further 5–10 minutes, until the potatoes are tender and golden brown. Cool and set aside.

2 Chop the chard stems and boil in water to soften for 5 minutes, then add the leaves, cover the pan and cook for 7–10 minutes until tender. Drain very well, then mix with the dolcelatte.

3 Turn the roulade out on to its covering piece of nonstick paper. Cover the surface with the chard mixture. Starting with one of the short edges, carefully roll up the roulade, using the paper underneath to help – it rolls up quite easily and you can be firm with it!

4 Put the roulade on to a heatproof serving dish. About 15 minutes before you want to serve it, pop the roulade back into the oven, uncovered, until heated through and crisp and golden on the outside. Serve at once, with a green salad.

This wonderful, unusual roulade can be made in advance, ready for reheating just before serving, when it will become crisp and gorgeous. A tomato sauce, such as the one on page 28, and fine green beans go well with it.

bubble-and-squeak cakes with beetroot relish

honey cabbage onion

serves 4
preparation 20 minutes, plus standing
cooking 30 minutes

1 kg (2 lb) potatoes, peeled and cut into even-sized pieces
40 g (1½ oz) butter
1 sweetheart or similar cabbage, shredded
6 spring onions, finely chopped
2–3 tablespoons wholemeal flour
olive oil for shallow-frying
salt and pepper, to taste
drizzle of olive oil and sprigs of dill, to garnish

for the beetroot relish
2 cooked beetroots, peeled and diced
2 tablespoons finely chopped onion
1 tablespoon clear honey
1 tablespoon cider vinegar

1 First make the relish. Put the beetroot into a bowl, stir in the onion, honey and cider vinegar and season with salt and pepper. Set aside for at least 30 minutes until needed – this relish improves with keeping: it's fine to make it several hours in advance if convenient.

2 Meanwhile, cover the potatoes in boiling water and cook for about 20 minutes, or until tender. Drain and mash with the butter.

3 Put the cabbage into 2 cm (1 inch) of boiling water, cover and cook until tender – about 6 minutes. Drain well, then add the cabbage to the potatoes, along with the spring onions and some salt and pepper.

4 Form the mixture into 4 large flat cakes. Just before you want to serve the cakes, coat them all over in flour, then immediately shallow-fry in sizzling hot olive oil until browned and crisp on both sides, flipping them over to cook the second side.

5 Serve at once, topping each one with a spoonful of beetroot relish, a drizzle of oil and sprigs of dill.

Sometimes the simplest things are best! I don't know what it is about these, but everyone loves them.

ricotta and plum tomato cake with pesto sauce

eggs tomatoes basil

serves 4
preparation 20 minutes
cooking 1¼ hours

4 x 250 g (8 oz) tubs ricotta cheese
175 g (6 oz) Parmesan-style cheese, finely grated
50 g (2 oz) butter, melted
2 eggs plus 2 egg yolks
2 large plum tomatoes, about 250 g (8 oz), sliced into rounds
bunch of basil, torn
salt and pepper, to taste
25 g (1 oz) toasted pine nuts and basil leaves, to garnish

for the sauce
4 tablespoons pesto
4 tablespoons water

1 Put the ricotta, Parmesan, butter, whole eggs and egg yolks into a food processor and whiz to a smooth cream. Season with salt and pepper.

2 Spoon half the ricotta mixture into the base of a 22 cm (8½ inch) springform tin. Arrange the tomatoes on top and scatter with torn basil and some salt and pepper. Gently spoon the rest of the ricotta mixture on top.

3 Bake in a preheated oven, 190°C (375°F), Gas Mark 5, for 1–1¼ hours, or until risen and lightly browned, firm to touch and a skewer inserted into the centre comes out clean – cover the top lightly with a piece of foil if it starts to get too brown.

4 Remove from the oven and leave to stand for 5 minutes to settle, then remove the sides of the tin and put the cake on to a warm serving dish.

5 To make the sauce, mix the pesto and water. Drizzle some of this over the top of the cake and serve the rest in a small bowl. Scatter the top of the cake with pine nuts and basil leaves and serve at once.

refritos gateau

beans avocado cream

serves 4
preparation 20 minutes
cooking 35–40 minutes

2 onions, chopped
2 tablespoons olive oil
1 green chilli, deseeded and chopped
4 garlic cloves, crushed
4 x 425 g (14 oz) cans red kidney beans, drained and rinsed
4 tablespoons tomato purée
2 eggs
salt and pepper, to taste

to assemble and garnish
220 g (7½ oz) jar tomato salsa
175 g (6 oz) grated Cheddar cheese
1 large avocado
2 x 142 g (4½ oz) pots soured cream
a little chopped red pepper
1–2 tablespoons chopped fresh coriander
100 g (3½ oz) packet plain tortilla chips

1 Fry the onions in the olive oil in a large saucepan for about 10 minutes, or until tender. Add the green chilli and garlic and cook for a further 1–2 minutes.

2 Remove from the heat and add the beans, mashing them to make a chunky mixture that holds together. Stir in the tomato purée and eggs and season with salt and pepper.

3 Line 2 x 20 cm (8 inch) round loose-based tins with nonstick paper. Divide the mixture between them and bake in a preheated oven, 180°C (350°F), Gas Mark 4, for 25 minutes, or until firm in the centre.

4 Turn one of the bean cakes out on to an ovenproof plate and strip off the lining paper. Spread about 4 tablespoons of the salsa on top, then cover with the Cheddar. Turn out the second bean cake, strip off the lining paper and place the cake on top of the cheese, pressing down firmly but gently. If not serving immediately, cover with foil and place in the oven until just before you want to serve it – the cheese layer will melt a bit.

5 To serve, peel the avocado and cut into long slices. Cover the top of the cake with soured cream, letting it drizzle down the sides. Arrange the slices of avocado on the cream and scatter with chopped red pepper and coriander. Stick a few tortilla chips jauntily in the top (serve the rest in a bowl) and serve at once.

A gateau of refritos – Mexican refried beans – makes a luscious and dramatic centrepiece dish.

bean, beer and vegetable puff pie

leeks celery pastry

serves 4
preparation 30 minutes, plus cooling
cooking 1 hour

2 tablespoons olive oil
2 onions, finely chopped
2 celery sticks, sliced
3 garlic cloves, chopped
1½ tablespoons plain white flour
300 ml (½ pint) vegetable stock
150 ml (¼ pint) beer
1 tablespoon shoyu or tamari
2 teaspoons ready-made mustard
450 g (14½ oz) carrots, sliced
450 g (14½ oz) leeks, cut into 2.5 cm (1 inch) lengths
250 g (8 oz) baby onions, halved or quartered
425 g (14 oz) can butterbeans, drained and rinsed
1–2 tablespoons caster sugar
375 g (12 oz) frozen ready-rolled all-butter puff pastry (see page 184)
salt and pepper, to taste

1 Heat the olive oil in a large saucepan, add the chopped onions and celery and stir, then cover and leave to cook gently for 7–8 minutes, until tender but not browned. Stir in the garlic and cook for a further minute or so.

2 Sprinkle in the flour and stir over the heat for 1–2 minutes until the flour turns nut-brown. Pour in the stock and beer and stir over the heat until the mixture has thickened slightly.

3 Stir in the shoyu or tamari, the mustard and some salt and pepper, then add the carrots, leeks and baby onions. Bring to the boil, then reduce the heat, cover the pan and cook gently for about 25 minutes, or until the vegetables are tender. Add the butterbeans and sugar and season with salt and pepper, then set aside to cool.

4 Transfer the vegetable mixture to a shallow pie dish. Measure the pastry against the dish, cut off the excess and cut this into long thin strips. Brush the rim of the pie dish and the long strips of pastry with a little cold water. Press the strips all round the rim of the dish. Ease the pastry on top of the pie, so that it rests on the pastry-covered rim of the dish. Press the edges of the pastry, decorate as desired and make a steam-hole in the centre.

5 Bake the pie in a preheated oven, 200°C (400°F), Gas Mark 6, for 20 minutes, or until the pastry is puffy and golden brown. Serve at once.

This old-fashioned homely dish goes well with mashed potatoes and a cooked green vegetable, such as cabbage or Brussels sprouts.

stilton, apple and sage crêpes with berry sauce

apples port stilton

serves 4
preparation 30 minutes
cooking 30 minutes

250 g (8 oz) shallots, chopped
1 tablespoon olive oil
375 g (12 oz) apples, peeled and chopped
50 g (2 oz) fine fresh white breadcrumbs
150 g (5 oz) Stilton cheese, crumbled
1 tablespoon chopped sage
8 crêpes, made according to the pancake recipe on page 158, omitting sugar, or shop-bought crêpes
2 eggs, beaten
dry polenta for coating
rapeseed or groundnut oil for deep-frying
salt and pepper, to taste
red chard leaves, to garnish

for the blackberry sauce
4 tablespoons blackberry jelly or jam
1 teaspoon Dijon mustard
2 tablespoons each freshly squeezed orange and lemon juice
4 tablespoons port

1 Fry the shallots in the olive oil for 5 minutes, then add the apples, cover and cook for a further 5–10 minutes, or until the shallots and apples are tender. Remove from the heat and add the breadcrumbs, Stilton and sage, then season with salt and pepper.

2 Put a spoonful of the filling towards the edge of a crêpe. Fold the sides over it and roll up, as if wrapping a parcel. Continue until all the crêpes and filling are used. Carefully dip each crêpe in beaten egg, then into polenta, to coat completely. Put the coated crêpes on a piece of nonstick paper and chill until required.

3 To make the sauce, mix all the ingredients in a small saucepan and simmer over a moderate heat for 4–5 minutes until glossy and syrupy. Pour into a jug to serve.

4 Heat the oil to 180–190°C (350–375°F), or until a cube of bread browns in 30 seconds. Deep-fry the crêpes until crisp and golden brown, then drain on kitchen paper. To serve, pour a little sauce on each plate, add a crêpe or 2 and garnish with a red chard leaf.

brie and cranberry soufflés

cheddar brie eggs

serves 4
preparation 30 minutes
cooking 40 minutes

for the cranberry sauce
175 g (6 oz) cranberries
125 g (4 oz) caster sugar

for the soufflés
15 g (½ oz) butter, plus extra for greasing the dish
1 tablespoon plain white flour
100 ml (3½ fl oz) milk
1 teaspoon Dijon mustard
40 g (1½ oz) grated Cheddar cheese
pinch of white pepper
3 egg whites
2 egg yolks
100 g (3½ oz) Brie cheese, not too ripe, thinly sliced
salt, to taste

1 First make the cranberry sauce. Wash the cranberries and put them, with just the water clinging to them, into a saucepan and heat gently for 10 minutes, or until they're soft. Add the sugar and simmer gently for about 15 minutes, or until 'jammy'. Set aside.

2 Melt the butter in a saucepan and stir in the flour. Cook for a minute, stirring, then remove from the heat and gradually stir in the milk. Bring to the boil and cook, stirring, until the sauce thickens, then remove from the heat and stir in the mustard, Cheddar, white pepper and a little salt. Leave to cool slightly.

3 Whisk the egg whites until they stand in soft peaks. Stir the egg yolks into the cheese mixture, then stir in 1 tablespoon of the whisked whites to loosen the mixture. Gently fold in the rest of the egg whites.

4 Generously grease 4 x 150 ml (¼ pint) ramekins or individual soufflé dishes. Put 1 tablespoon of the mixture into each dish, then cover with 1–2 slices of Brie and 1–2 teaspoons of the cranberry sauce. Spoon the rest of the soufflé mixture on top – it can come to the top of the dishes but no higher.

5 Stand the dishes in a roasting tin, pour in boiling water to come halfway up the sides and bake in a preheated oven, 180°C (350°F), Gas Mark 4, for 13–15 minutes until risen and golden brown and a skewer inserted into the centre of a soufflé comes out clean. Serve at once.

You won't need the full quantity of cranberry sauce for this, but it's not worth making less – serve the remainder with the soufflés, or keep it in a jar in the refrigerator for up to 4 weeks.

individual pea, spinach and mint pithiviers

spinach cream pastry

serves 4
preparation 25 minutes
cooking 30 minutes

250 g (8 oz) baby spinach leaves
200 g (7 oz) frozen petit pois, thawed
4 tablespoons chopped mint
375 g (12 oz) frozen ready-rolled all-butter puff pastry (see page 184)
200 g (7 oz) Boursin garlic and herb cream cheese
4 tablespoons cream, to glaze
salt and pepper, to taste

1 Cook the spinach in a dry saucepan for 1–2 minutes until wilted, then drain and cool. Season with salt and pepper. Mash the peas with the mint – give them a quick whiz in a food processor or with a stick blender – so they hold together a bit.

2 Lay the pastry on a board and roll to make it even thinner, then cut into 4 x 10 cm (4 inch) circles for the bases, and 4 slightly larger ones, about 17 cm (6¾ inch) (a saucer is useful for cutting round) to go over the top.

3 Place the smaller circles on a baking sheet. Put a layer of spinach on top of each circle, leaving about 1 cm (½ inch) free round the edges. Put a quarter of the Boursin on top of the spinach, then heap the peas on top and around the Boursin. Cover with the remaining pastry circles, pressing the edges neatly together and crimping with your fingers or the prongs of a fork. Make a hole in the centre of each and decorate the top with little cuts spiralling out from the centre, like a traditional pithiviers, if you wish. All this can be done in advance. When ready to cook, brush the tops with the cream.

4 Bake the pithiviers in a preheated oven, 200°C (400°F), Gas Mark 6, for about 25 minutes, or until puffed up, golden brown and crisp. Serve at once.

tofu braised with herbs and red wine

parsley tofu thyme

V

serves 4
preparation 10 minutes, plus marinating
cooking 45 minutes

2 x 250 g (8 oz) blocks firm tofu, drained
4 tablespoons ketjap manis (see page 184) or soy sauce
2–3 tablespoons olive oil
2 onions, sliced into rounds
2 carrots, sliced into slim batons
200 g (7 oz) turnips, diced
2 garlic cloves, finely chopped
2 tablespoons brandy
150 ml (¼ pint) red wine
450 ml (¾ pint) vegetable stock
small bunch of fresh thyme
sugar, salt and pepper, to taste
chopped parsley, to serve

1 Cut the tofu in half, then cut each slice in half widthways, to make 8 'steaks'. Lay these on a large shallow plate or container and pour over the ketjap manis or soy sauce, turning the pieces of tofu so that they are coated all over. Set aside to marinate for 30 minutes.

2 Drain the tofu, reserving the liquid. Heat 2 tablespoons of the olive oil in a large shallow frying pan or sauté pan, add the tofu and fry on both sides until well browned. Remove from the pan, add another tablespoon of olive oil, if necessary, and add the onions, carrots and turnips. Fry for 10 minutes, browning lightly.

3 Add the tofu and its reserved liquid and the garlic to the pan with the brandy, wine, stock, thyme, about 1 teaspoon of sugar and some salt and pepper. Let the mixture simmer gently for about 30 minutes, or until all the vegetables are meltingly tender and bathed in a syrupy glaze. Serve from the pan, topped with a little chopped parsley.

Braising tofu in traditional French style is a great way to pack it with flavour and delectable juices. It's wonderful with creamy potatoes and a lightly cooked green vegetable or salad.

smoked tofu with peanuts and coconut rice

rice chilli coconut

serves 4
preparation 20 minutes
cooking 30 minutes

2 x 220 g (7½ oz) blocks smoked tofu, drained
75 g (3 oz) chunky peanut butter
1 teaspoon grated fresh root ginger
2 garlic cloves, crushed
4 teaspoons shoyu or tamari, plus extra for finishing
chickpea flour for coating
olive oil, for frying
chopped fresh coriander, to garnish
sweet chilli sauce, to serve

for the coconut rice
1 tablespoon toasted sesame oil
350 g (11½ oz) white basmati rice
300 ml (½ pint) water
400 g (13 oz) can organic coconut milk
2 lemon grass stalks, crushed
½ teaspoon salt

1 Start with the rice. Heat the sesame oil in a saucepan, add the rice and stir over the heat for 3–4 minutes, until translucent. Add the water, coconut milk, lemon grass and salt. Bring to the boil, cover and cook over a very gentle heat for 12 minutes. Remove from the heat and leave with the lid on to stand for 5 minutes. Remove the lemon grass and fluff the rice with a fork.

2 Halve the blocks of tofu horizontally, to make 4 thin slices.

3 Mix the peanut butter with the ginger, garlic and 4 teaspoons of shoyu or tamari, to make a thick paste. Spread a little on one side of each of the pieces of tofu, taking it right to the edges.

4 Sandwich the tofu in pairs, putting the peanut-coated surfaces together – coating both sides helps the pieces to stick firmly.

5 Cut each sandwich into fingers, making 8 long ones, or shorter ones if you prefer. Drizzle a little shoyu or tamari on each side of each of these fingers, then dip them in chickpea flour to coat all sides.

6 Shallow-fry the fingers in hot olive oil until crisp and golden brown, turning them to cook both sides.

7 Put the rice on to a large warm serving platter. Arrange the tofu fingers on top and scatter with chopped coriander. Serve with sweet chilli sauce.

wild mushroom tempura with garlic mayonnaise

mayo oil mushroom

V

serves 4
preparation 15 minutes
cooking 30 minutes

500 g (1 lb) mixed wild mushrooms, torn into bite-sized pieces
rapeseed or groundnut oil, for deep-frying
garlic mayonnaise or aioli, to serve

for the tempura batter
100 g (3½ oz) plain white flour
200 g (7 oz) cornflour
3 teaspoons baking powder
200 ml (7 fl oz) sparkling water
salt, to taste

1 Just before you want to serve the mushrooms, heat sufficient oil for deep-frying in a deep-fat fryer to 180–190°C (350–375°F), or until a cube of bread browns in 30 seconds.

2 While the oil is heating, make the batter. Put the flour, cornflour and baking powder into a bowl with some salt. Pour in the water and stir the mixture quickly with a fork or chopstick to make a batter.

3 Dip pieces of mushroom into the batter, then put them into the hot oil for 1–2 minutes until they are golden brown and very crisp. Lift them out on to kitchen paper. You will need to do a number of batches, but the first ones will keep crisp while you do the rest.

4 Pile the tempura on a plate and serve immediately with the garlic mayonnaise or aioli.

Provided you buy a vegan mayonnaise, this makes a luxurious vegan main course – the unusual tempura batter is light and very crisp. A bag of mixed wild mushrooms from a supermarket is perfect for this recipe.

portobello steaks en croûte

brandy garlic cream

serves 4
preparation 10 minutes
cooking 25 minutes

4 portobello mushrooms
4 garlic cloves, chopped
4 teaspoons brandy
90 g (3½ oz) jar vegetarian tapenade, green or black
375 g (12 oz) frozen ready-rolled all-butter puff pastry (see page 184)
4–6 tablespoons cream or soya cream, to glaze
salt and pepper, to taste

1 Sit the mushrooms stem-side up and make crisscross cuts all over the stem-tops and surface, being careful not to cut right through the base of the mushroom.

2 Rub the garlic into the cuts, along with the brandy and some salt and pepper, then top each with a generous amount of tapenade, dividing the jar between them.

3 Spread out the pastry on a floured board and roll it a bit to make it as thin as you can. Cut it into 4 pieces – they will be roughly square.

4 Put a mushroom stem-side up into the centre of each pastry square and fold the sides up to encase it, but not completely cover the top. Put the mushroom parcels on to a baking sheet and brush the sides and top of the pastry with cream.

5 Bake in a preheated oven, 200°C (400°F), Gas Mark 6, for 25 minutes, or until the pastry is puffed up and golden brown and the mushrooms are tender.

Braised Whole Baby Carrots and Fennel (see page 44) together with Saffron and Garlic Mash (see page 47) would go well with this.

aubergine schnitzels with watercress sauce

arame tofu cream

serves 4
preparation 30 minutes, plus soaking
cooking 25 minutes

5 g (¼ oz) arame seaweed
2 aubergines, stems trimmed
olive oil for brushing and shallow-frying
220 g (7½ oz) block smoked tofu, drained
6 tablespoons cornflour
5 tablespoons water
25 g (1 oz) dried breadcrumbs
salt and pepper, to taste
lemon slices, to serve

for the watercress sauce
bunch or packet of watercress
200 ml (7 fl oz) single cream or unsweetened soya cream
1 teaspoon cornflour

1 Cover the arame with cold water and leave to soak for 10 minutes.

2 Meanwhile, cut the aubergines lengthways into 4 slices – or in half, then in half again. (Two of the slices will have skin on one side.) Brush the cut surfaces of the aubergine with olive oil, place on a grill pan and cook under a hot grill until they are lightly browned and feel tender to the point of a knife, turning them over when the first side is done.

3 Whiz the tofu and arame to a purée in a food processor or using a stick blender. Season with salt and pepper, then spread some of the mixture thickly on one slice of aubergine and press another slice on top to make a fat sandwich. Repeat with all the slices, dividing the tofu mixture evenly between them.

4 Put the cornflour into a bowl and mix in the water to make a thick coating paste. Dip each aubergine sandwich into the paste, then into the breadcrumbs, making sure it's thoroughly coated. Shallow-fry the schnitzels on both sides in hot olive oil, drain on kitchen paper and serve garnished with slices of lemon and accompanied by the watercress sauce.

5 To make the sauce, whiz the watercress, cream and cornflour to a purée in a food processor or using a stick blender. Heat gently, stirring, until thickened.

Thick slices of grilled aubergine sandwiched with smoked tofu and arame – a delicately flavoured seaweed – give these schnitzels a gorgeous juiciness and smoky flavour, encased in a crisp crumb coating.

lemon-glazed and seared halloumi with herb salad

honey herbs lemon

serves 4
preparation 10 minutes, plus marinating
cooking 5–10 minutes

2 x 250 g (8 oz) packets halloumi cheese, drained
4 tablespoons freshly squeezed lemon juice
2 tablespoons clear honey

for the herb salad
250 g (8 oz) mixed baby leaves and herb salad
2 tablespoons olive oil
salt and pepper, to taste

1 Cut the halloumi into slices about 5 mm (¼ inch) thick. Put them on a plate in a single layer.

2 Mix the lemon juice with the honey and pour over the halloumi, turning it to coat the slices all over. Set aside for at least 1 hour.

3 When you are ready to serve, toss the leaves with the olive oil and some salt and pepper and divide between 4 plates.

4 Put the slices of halloumi into a dry frying pan over a moderate heat, reserving any liquid. Fry on one side until golden brown, then flip them over and fry the second side. This is a very quick process as they cook fast. When the second sides are done, pour in any liquid that was left and let it bubble up until it has mostly evaporated and becomes a sweet glaze.

5 Arrange the slices of halloumi on top of the salad and serve at once.

The halloumi can be marinated well in advance, but cook it quickly at the last minute so that it is light and delicious.

lentil cakes in citrus broth

lime lentils onion

serves 4
preparation 1 hour
cooking 45–50 minutes

for the lentil cakes
350 g (11½ oz) Puy lentils
1 onion, roughly chopped
900 ml (1½ pints) water
20 g (¾ oz) packet fresh coriander, chopped
1 tablespoon ground coriander
juice of 1½ limes
olive oil for shallow-frying
salt and pepper, to taste

for the broth
600 ml (1 pint) vegetable stock
2 lemon grass stalks, crushed
green tops from a bunch of spring onions
3–4 kaffir lime leaves
2 garlic cloves
20 g (¾ oz) packet fresh coriander, chopped

1 Put the lentils into a saucepan with the onion and water. Bring to the boil, then reduce the heat, cover the pan and simmer very gently for 40–45 minutes, or until the lentils are very tender and all the water has been absorbed. Add a little more water towards the end of cooking if the lentils are sticking, but make sure no water remains.

2 Mash the lentils with the fresh and ground coriander, the lime juice and some salt and pepper. Form into 12 cakes, pressing the mixture so it holds together. Fry the lentil cakes in a little hot olive oil until crisp and browned on both sides.

3 To make the broth, put the stock into a saucepan with the lemon grass, spring onion tops, lime leaves and garlic. Bring to the boil, then reduce the heat and simmer, uncovered, for a few minutes, until the liquid has reduced by half. Strain, discard the flavourings and return the stock to the pan with the chopped coriander.

4 Serve the lentil cakes in shallow bowls in a pool of the broth. Cabbage with Sesame and Ginger (see page 46) would go well with this.

carrot, parsnip and chestnut terrine with red wine gravy

fennel eggs wine

serves 4
preparation 30 minutes
cooking 1 hour 5 minutes

3 garlic cloves, chopped
50 g (2 oz) butter
2 tablespoons dried breadcrumbs
2 tablespoons olive oil
2 onions, chopped
200 g (7 oz) parsnips, cut into 1 cm (½ inch) chunks
200 g (7 oz) carrots, sliced into rounds
200 g (7 oz) trimmed fennel, chopped
1 teaspoon caraway seeds
200 g (7 oz) vacuum pack whole peeled chestnuts
75 g (3 oz) fine soft wholemeal breadcrumbs
4 tablespoons lemon juice
2 tablespoons shoyu or tamari
3 eggs, beaten
2 tablespoons chopped parsley
salt and pepper, to taste

for the red wine gravy
2 onions, finely chopped
1 tablespoon olive oil
2 tablespoons plain white flour
200 ml (7 fl oz) vegetable stock
200 ml (7 fl oz) red wine
2 tablespoons shoyu or tamari
sugar, to taste

1 Line a 900 g (1 lb 13 oz) loaf tin with a strip of nonstick paper. Mix the garlic with the butter and use half of this to grease the lined base and sides of the tin, then coat the base and sides with half the dried breadcrumbs.

2 Heat the olive oil in a large saucepan and add the onions, parsnips, carrots and fennel. Cover and cook very gently for about 20 minutes, stirring from time to time, or until all the vegetables are tender.

3 Add the caraway seeds and cook for 1–2 minutes longer, then remove from the heat and mix in the chestnuts, soft breadcrumbs, lemon juice, shoyu or tamari, the eggs, parsley and some salt and pepper.

4 Spoon the mixture into the prepared loaf tin and level the surface. Scatter the top with the rest of the dried breadcrumbs and dot with the remaining garlic butter. Bake in a preheated oven, 180°C (350°F), Gas Mark 4, for 40 minutes, until firm on top and a skewer inserted into the centre comes out clean.

5 While the loaf is cooking, make the gravy. Fry the onions in the olive oil for 10 minutes, until they are tender and lightly browned. Add the flour and stir over the heat for 3–4 minutes, until nut-brown – the mixture will be very dry. Stir in the stock and wine, then simmer over a moderate heat until thickened. Add the shoyu or tamari and season with salt, pepper and perhaps a touch of sugar. Serve as it is or, if you prefer smooth gravy, strain it through a sieve. Either way, add more stock if you want it thinner.

6 Serve the terrine in thick slices with the red wine gravy.

toover dhal with lime and coriander leaf dumplings

cloves cumin lime

serves 4
preparation 20 minutes
cooking 1¼ hours

for the dhal

350 g (11½ oz) toover (toor) dhal (see page 185), thoroughly washed in hot water and drained
2 litres (3½ pints) water
2 tablespoons olive oil
2 whole cloves
1 cinnamon stick
1–2 dried red chillies
6 dried kaffir lime leaves
1 whole green chilli
400 g (13 oz) can chopped tomatoes
1 tablespoon garam masala
1 tablespoon freshly squeezed lemon juice
sugar, salt and pepper, to taste

for the coriander dumplings

125 g (4 oz) self-raising flour
2 teaspoons cumin seeds
20 g (¾ oz) packet fresh coriander, chopped
finely grated rind of 1 lime
4 tablespoons olive oil
4 tablespoons water

1 Put the toover dhal into a large saucepan with the water and bring to the boil. Using a perforated spoon, scoop off the foam, then reduce the heat, cover the pan and leave to cook very gently for about 1 hour, until very soft.

2 Meanwhile, heat the olive oil in a medium saucepan and add the cloves, cinnamon stick and dried chillies. Let them sizzle for about half a minute, then add the lime leaves and sizzle again. Stir in the green chilli, cook for a few more seconds, then add the tomatoes. Bring to the boil, then reduce the heat and leave to simmer, uncovered, for 15–20 minutes, or until very thick, stirring often to prevent sticking. Remove the cinnamon stick, chilli and any large pieces of lime leaf.

3 Stir the dhal to give a creamy consistency, then add the tomato mixture, garam masala, lemon juice, ½–1 tablespoon sugar and some salt and pepper.

4 To make the dumplings, put the flour into a bowl, add all the remaining ingredients with salt to taste, and mix quickly to a soft dough. Form into 8 dumplings. Bring the dhal to a gentle boil and drop in the dumplings. Reduce the heat, cover the pan and cook for about 15 minutes, or until the dumplings have risen to the surface and are cooked inside. Serve from the pot or carefully transfer to a warmed casserole.

The dumplings are very British, but with the fresh Asian flavourings they seem made to go with this dish perfectly.

decadent desserts and cakes

For a special, memorable meal, a gorgeous pudding or cake reawakens people's interest after the delights of the main course and provides the final drama. Here is a varied selection of delights for your 'closing act', designed to satisfy all tastes and, who knows, even evoke a round of applause …

melting chocolate puddings

vanilla eggs cocoa

serves 4
preparation 25 minutes
cooking 20 minutes

50 g (2 oz) butter, plus extra for greasing
100 g (3½ oz) plain chocolate, broken
2 eggs
50 g (2 oz) caster sugar
½ teaspoon vanilla extract
1 tablespoon plain white flour
8 squares, 25–50 g (1–2 oz) good-quality white chocolate
cocoa powder for dusting
thick cream, to serve

1 Line 4 x 150 ml (¼ pint) individual metal pudding basins with a disc of nonstick paper in the base and butter them very thoroughly.

2 Put the plain chocolate and butter into a heatproof bowl set over a pan of gently steaming water and leave to melt, then stir, remove from the heat and leave to cool slightly.

3 Using an electric whisk, beat together the eggs, sugar and vanilla extract until very thick and pale – this takes at least 5 minutes.

4 Gently fold the melted chocolate and flour into the whisked mixture until completely incorporated. Put 1 tablespoon of the chocolate mixture into each pudding basin and put them into a preheated oven, 200°C (400°F), Gas Mark 6, for 5 minutes, then remove them and quickly fill the basins with the rest of the mixture. Drop 2 squares of the white chocolate into each. Put them back into the oven and bake for 11–12 minutes, or until risen and a bit crusty around the edges.

5 Remove from the oven and leave to stand for 1–2 minutes, then slip a knife around the sides and invert each pudding over a warmed plate. Leave for another 30 seconds, then gently lift off the pudding basins. Dust the puddings with a little cocoa powder and serve immediately with thick cream.

Little melting chocolate puddings have become a modern classic – and these provide a new twist because when you cut them open, white chocolate oozes out! They are easy to do and can be prepared well in advance, ready for cooking just before serving.

little plum upside-down puddings with cinnamon custard

plums sugar milk

serves 4
preparation 30 minutes
cooking 30 minutes

butter, for greasing
125 g (4 oz) caster sugar, plus more as required
500 g (1 lb) plums, sliced and stones removed
4 tablespoons water

for the sponge
2 eggs
50 g (2 oz) caster sugar
50 g (2 oz) self-raising flour

for the custard
2 egg yolks
1 teaspoon cornflour
1 tablespoon caster sugar
300 ml (½ pint) creamy milk
½ cinnamon stick

1 Line a baking sheet with nonstick paper, grease generously with butter and place 4 x 10 cm (4 inch) chefs' rings on it. Sprinkle inside the rings lightly with some of the sugar.

2 Put the plums into a saucepan with the rest of the sugar and the water. Cover and cook over a moderate heat for 3–4 minutes, or until the plums are just tender but not collapsed. Remove from the heat. Taste and add more sugar if necessary.

3 To make the sponge, whisk the eggs and sugar together until very thick and pale – this takes about 5 minutes with an electric whisk. Sift the flour over the top and fold in gently with a spatula.

4 Divide the plums between the rings, spreading them out so that they cover the whole area. Spoon the sponge mixture on top, levelling it off. Bake in a preheated oven, 180°C (350°F), Gas Mark 4, for 20 minutes, or until the sponge springs back when touched lightly in the centre.

5 To make the custard, put the egg yolks, cornflour and sugar into a bowl and whisk together. Pour the milk into a saucepan, add the cinnamon stick and bring to the boil. Gradually whisk the hot milk into the egg mixture, then return the mixture to the pan and stir over a gentle heat for a few minutes until the mixture thickens and will coat the back of a spoon. Remove the cinnamon stick. The custard can be served hot or cold.

6 Run a knife around the edges of the rings, then turn each pudding out on to a warmed serving plate. Pour a little of the custard around, and serve the rest in a jug.

Chefs' rings are ideal for making these, but if you don't have any, you could use 10 cm (4 inch) loose-based shallow flan tins lined with a circle of nonstick paper.

pear and brioche charlotte

vanilla pears butter

serves 4
preparation 25 minutes
cooking 1¼ hours

750 g (1½ lb) pears, peeled, cored and cut into pieces
2 tablespoons caster sugar
2 tablespoons water
1 vanilla pod
8–10 slices of brioche
125 g (4 oz) butter, melted
250 g (8 oz) tub mascarpone cheese
2 egg yolks
2 tablespoons demerara sugar
thick pouring cream, to serve (optional)

1 Put the pears into a saucepan with the caster sugar, water and vanilla pod. Bring to the boil, then reduce the heat, cover the pan and leave to cook very gently for about 30 minutes, or until the pears are very tender. Set aside until completely cold.

2 Brush the slices of brioche with the melted butter and arrange them in a 20 cm (8 inch) sponge sandwich cake tin with a removable base, or a shallow ovenproof casserole, covering the base and sides and saving some slices for the top.

3 Beat the mascarpone a little to soften. Mix in the egg yolks and the pears together with any liquid. Spoon this on top of the brioche, then put the remaining brioche slices on top, brush with melted butter and sprinkle with demerara sugar.

4 Bake in a preheated oven, 180°C (350°F), Gas Mark 4, for about 40 minutes, or until the charlotte is golden, crisp and set in the middle – cover it with a piece of foil towards the end of the cooking time if it seems to be getting too crisp on top before the inside is set.

5 Serve hot, warm or cold, with pouring cream, if you wish.

banana and earl grey cake

tea eggs banana

serves 4
preparation 10 minutes, plus standing for the tea
cooking 30–35 minutes

8 Earl Grey tea bags
250 ml (8 fl oz) boiling water
1 large banana
125 g (4 oz) soft butter
125 g (4 oz) soft brown sugar
2 eggs
200 g (7 oz) self-raising flour
2 teaspoons baking powder

for the icing
175 g (6 oz) icing sugar
1 teaspoon butter
1 drop bergamot essential oil (optional)

1 Add the tea bags to the boiling water in a measuring jug, making sure they're all submerged. Cover with a plate and leave until cold.

2 Squeeze the tea bags to get as much liquid from them as possible, then discard the tea bags and measure out 150 ml (¼ pint) of tea. Put this tea into a food processor or mixer (reserve the rest). Peel and mash the banana and add to the tea with the butter, soft brown sugar, eggs, flour and baking powder, then whiz or beat until the mixture is light and fluffy.

3 Line an 18–20 cm (7–8 inch) cake tin with nonstick baking paper, spoon the mixture in and gently level the surface. Bake in a preheated oven, 180°C (350°F), Gas Mark 4, for 30–35 minutes, or until a skewer inserted into the centre comes out clean. Cool for a minute or so in the tin, then turn out on to a wire rack and leave until cold.

4 To make the icing, put the icing sugar into a saucepan with the butter, bergamot oil, if using, and 2 tablespoons of the remaining tea. Stir over the heat until the butter has melted. Pour over the top of the cake and leave to set.

The bergamot oil, which you can get at any healthfood shop, intensifies the flavour of the Earl Grey in this stylish cake.

lemon and almond drizzle cake with berries

almonds sugar lemon

serves 4
preparation 25 minutes, plus standing
cooking 40–45 minutes

175 g (6 oz) butter, softened
175 g (6 oz) caster sugar
2 eggs
finely grated rind of 1 lemon
175 g (6 oz) self-raising flour
50 g (2 oz) ground almonds
1½ teaspoons baking powder
crème fraîche, to serve

for the drizzle topping
4 tablespoons lemon juice
150 g (5 oz) icing sugar

for the berries
500 g (1 lb) mixed berries, such as raspberries, strawberries, blueberries or redcurrants, any stems and hulls removed
caster sugar, to taste

1 Line a 900 g (1 lb 13 oz) loaf tin with a strip of nonstick baking paper to cover the base and narrow sides.

2 Whisk together the butter, caster sugar, eggs and lemon rind until creamy, then stir in the flour, ground almonds and baking powder.

3 Spoon the cake mixture into the prepared loaf tin and gently level the top. Bake in a preheated oven, 160°C (325°F), Gas Mark 3, for 40–45 minutes, until risen and firm to a light touch and a skewer inserted into the centre comes out clean.

4 Five minutes before the cake is done, make the drizzle topping. Mix the lemon juice and icing sugar in a small saucepan, then stir over a gentle heat until the icing sugar has dissolved.

5 As soon as the cake comes out of the oven, prick the top all over and pour the icing sugar mixture over the top. Set aside to cool, then remove the cake from the tin and strip off the paper.

6 Prepare the fruit an hour or so before you want to eat. Put it into a bowl, sprinkle over caster sugar to taste and set aside for 1 hour, stirring from time to time. Taste and add a little more sugar if necessary. Serve the fruit and cake with a bowl of crème fraîche.

fig tarte tatin with ginger cream

ginger figs pastry

serves 4
preparation 25 minutes
cooking 30 minutes

325 g (11 oz) frozen ready-rolled all-butter puff pastry (see page 184)
40 g (1½ oz) butter
900 g (1 lb 13 oz) figs, halved
40 g (1½ oz) caster sugar
25 g (1 oz) toasted flaked almonds (optional)

for the ginger cream
275 ml (9 fl oz) double cream
3 pieces of preserved stem ginger, very finely chopped

1 Roll the pastry a little on a floured surface to make it a bit thinner if you can, then cut a circle to fit 1 cm (½ inch) larger than the top of a 20 cm (8 inch) tarte tatin pan or cake tin.

2 Melt the butter in the tarte tatin pan or in a frying pan. Add the figs, cut-side down, and the sugar. Cook over a high heat for about 6 minutes, until the figs are slightly browned and caramelized.

3 If you're using a cake tin, put the figs, cut-side down, into it and scrape in all the gooey juice from the pan.

4 Put the pastry on top, tucking it down into the figs at the sides. Prick the pastry, then bake in a preheated oven, 200°C (400°F), Gas Mark 6, for 20–25 minutes, until crisp and golden brown.

5 Meanwhile, make the ginger cream. Whisk the cream until it is standing in soft peaks, then fold in the ginger. Transfer to a bowl and chill until required.

6 To serve, loosen the tarte with a knife, then invert over a plate. The figs will be on top. Scatter with toasted flaked almonds, if using, then leave to settle for a couple of minutes before serving with the ginger cream.

This is also delicious made with apricots. Make exactly as described, using 900 g (1 lb 13 oz) apricots, halved and stoned, instead of the figs.

orange creams with caramel and toffee sauce

sugar orange butter

serves 4
preparation 30 minutes, plus cooling
cooking 35 minutes

for the orange creams
300 ml (½ pint) double cream
2 pieces of pared orange rind
6 egg yolks
75 g (3 oz) caster sugar

for the oranges
4 ripe sweet juicy oranges
caster sugar, to taste

for the toffee sauce
50 g (2 oz) butter
5 tablespoons double cream
4 tablespoons soft brown sugar

1 Line the base of 4 ramekins with discs of nonstick paper.

2 Put the cream and orange rind into a saucepan and bring to the boil. Remove from the heat and allow to cool slightly. Remove the orange rind.

3 Whisk together the egg yolks and 25 g (1 oz) of the caster sugar to blend, then gradually whisk in the cream. Pour the mixture into the ramekins, stand them in a roasting tin and pour in boiling water to come half to three-quarters of the way up the sides of the ramekins. Bake in a preheated oven, 140°C (275°F), Gas Mark 1, for about 30 minutes, or until the custards are just firm in the centres. Remove from the oven, cool, then chill.

4 Cut the skin and pith from the oranges, then cut the segments out of the white inner skin. Put the segments into a bowl with a little caster sugar to taste if necessary and chill until required.

5 For the sauce, put the butter, cream and soft brown sugar into a saucepan and heat gently for 2–3 minutes, to make a golden toffee sauce.

6 To serve, loosen the sides of the orange creams and turn one out on to each plate, then remove the lining paper. Top each with a thin layer of the remaining caster sugar and heat with a cook's blowtorch to make a hard glazed golden topping. Alternatively, turn them out on to a heatproof plate that will fit under your grill, top each with a thin layer of caster sugar and grill them for 1–2 minutes to make the caramel, then carefully transfer each to a serving plate. Arrange some orange slices on each plate and drizzle some toffee sauce around the oranges. Serve at once.

This is a great mixture of flavours and textures. The orange creams can be topped with crisp shiny golden caramel if you have a cook's blowtorch, or you can place them under the grill – either way, they're delectable.

individual pavlovas with pomegranate and grenadine

cream grenadine eggs

serves 4
preparation 15 minutes, plus standing
cooking 40 minutes

2 egg whites
125 g (4 oz) caster sugar
1 teaspoon cornflour
¼ teaspoon vinegar

for the filling
seeds from 2 ripe pomegranates
4 tablespoons grenadine
300 ml (½ pint) double cream, whipped

1 Put the egg whites into a large, clean bowl and whisk until they are thick, glossy and standing in peaks. Whisk in the sugar 1 tablespoon at a time, then fold in the cornflour and vinegar.

2 Spoon the meringue on to a large baking sheet lined with nonstick paper, making 4 saucer-sized circles, and hollow each out in the centre a little. Bake in a preheated oven, 140°C (275°F), Gas Mark 1, for about 40 minutes, or until crisp on the outside but still soft within. Cool on the baking sheet.

3 While the pavlovas are cooking, put the pomegranate seeds into a small bowl with the grenadine and leave to steep.

4 To finish the pavlovas, spoon some whipped cream on to each, then top with the pomegranate seeds and their juice. Serve as soon as possible.

fruit sushi plate

vanilla lime fruit

serves 4
preparation 20 minutes, plus cooling
cooking 25 minutes

for the rice

175 g (6 oz) Japanese sushi rice or white 'pudding' rice
50 g (2 oz) caster sugar
400 g (13 oz) can organic coconut milk
1 vanilla pod
juice of 1 lime

for the fruit

125 g (4 oz) caster sugar
100 ml (3½ fl oz) water
1 lemon grass stalk, crushed
½ teaspoon dried red chilli flakes
juice and pared rind of 1 lime
1 carambola, thinly sliced
1 large ripe papaya, peeled, deseeded and sliced
2 kiwi fruits, peeled and sliced

1 Put the rice and sugar into a saucepan with the coconut milk and vanilla pod. Bring to the boil, then reduce the heat, cover the pan and leave to cook very gently for 20 minutes, or until the liquid has been absorbed and the rice is tender. Remove from the heat, gently stir in the lime juice and leave to cool.

2 Meanwhile, make an aromatic syrup for the fruit. Put the sugar and water in a saucepan with the lemon grass, chilli flakes and lime rind. Heat gently until the sugar has dissolved, then bring to the boil and remove from the heat.

3 Put the carambola in a single layer on a plate and pour the hot syrup over, together with the lemon grass and lime rind. Cover and leave until cold, then remove the lemon grass and lime rind, squeeze them to extract all the flavour and discard them. Sprinkle over the lime juice.

4 To serve, form the sweet sushi rice into small circles 2 cm (¾ inch) in diameter and 1 cm (½ inch) thick and arrange on plates. Top with carambola, papaya and kiwi fruit slices and spoon the syrup over them. Serve the remaining fruit on the side.

A plate of sweet sushi rice and lemon grass-scented fruits makes a very pretty and refreshing dessert.

coconut and kaffir lime panna cotta

cream lime coconut

serves 4
preparation 15 minutes, plus steeping and setting
cooking 10 minutes

400 g (13 oz) can organic coconut milk
150 ml (¼ pint) double cream
3 kaffir lime leaves
grated rind of 1 lime
2 tablespoons caster sugar
7 g (¼ oz) packet vegetarian gelatine (Vege-Gel, see page 185)
lime slices and fresh kaffir lime leaves (optional), to decorate

for the syrup
1 lemon grass stalk, crushed
juice and grated rind of 2 limes
6 tablespoons caster sugar

1 Put the coconut milk and cream into a saucepan with the lime leaves and lime rind. Bring to the boil, then cover, remove from the heat and set aside until cold.

2 Remove and discard the lime leaves. Stir in the sugar, then sprinkle the gelatine over the top, stirring all the time to prevent lumps. Heat gently, stirring all the time, until the mixture just reaches boiling point, then remove from the heat.

3 Pour the mixture into 4 x 125 ml (4 fl oz) ramekins or moulds and leave to set, but don't refrigerate.

4 To make the syrup, put the lemon grass, lime juice and rind and the sugar into a saucepan and heat gently to dissolve the sugar. Remove from the heat and set aside until required. Remove the lemon grass before serving.

5 Turn the panna cotta out on to individual serving plates and drizzle each with a little syrup. Decorate with slices of lime and lime leaves, if liked.

nectarines roasted with lavender

butter fruit sugar

serves 4
preparation 10 minutes
cooking 25 minutes

40 g (1½ oz) butter
3 tablespoons demerara sugar
2–3 dried heads of lavender
6 nectarines, halved and stones removed
chilled Greek yogurt, to serve

1 Select a shallow casserole dish that will hold all the nectarine halves in a single layer, grease generously with half the butter and sprinkle with half the sugar and half the lavender.

2 Place the nectarine halves, cut-side down, in the buttered casserole, dot with the rest of the butter and sprinkle with the remaining sugar and lavender.

3 Bake, uncovered, in a preheated oven, 180°C (350°F), Gas Mark 4, for about 25 minutes, or until the nectarines are tender. Serve hot or warm, with some chilled Greek yogurt.

The wonderful taste of summer on a plate – and so easy to do.

strawberries in rose jelly

berries juice sugar

V

serves 4
preparation 15 minutes, plus setting
cooking 5 minutes

4 tablespoons caster sugar
300 ml (½ pint) raspberry and cranberry juice
7 g (¼ oz) packet vegetarian gelatine (Vege-Gel, see page 185)
4 tablespoons rosewater
450 g (14½ oz) strawberries, hulled and sliced

1 Put the sugar into a saucepan with the raspberry and cranberry juice. Sprinkle the gelatine over the top, stirring all the time to avoid lumps. Heat gently, stirring, until the sugar has dissolved, then bring to the boil, boil for a few seconds and remove from the heat. Add the rosewater.

2 Blot the strawberries well on kitchen paper to dry them a bit, then divide between 4 glass dishes. Pour the jelly over the strawberries and leave to cool for an hour or so.

3 The mixture sets very quickly and needs to be eaten within a couple of hours, before the juice from the strawberries softens the jelly too much. If this happens, it still tastes good, but is not very jellied. Don't put it into the refrigerator or the jelly will become opaque.

sangria fruit salad with almond shortbreads

wine grapes brandy

serves 4
preparation 10 minutes, plus standing
cooking 15–20 minutes

juice and finely grated rind of 1 orange
4 tablespoons caster sugar
4 tablespoons red Spanish wine
1 tablespoon brandy
1 tablespoon Cointreau
2 oranges, skin and pith removed, cut into segments
1 apple, peeled and sliced
2 peaches, thinly sliced, stones removed
175 g (6 oz) white grapes, halved and any seeds removed
sprigs of fresh mint

for the shortbreads
175 g (6 oz) butter
50 g (2 oz) caster sugar
175 g (6 oz) plain white flour
50 g (2 oz) ground almonds
icing sugar, to serve

1 Put the orange juice and rind into a large bowl with the caster sugar, wine, brandy and Cointreau. Add all the prepared fruit and some of the mint sprigs and stir gently, then set aside for at least 30 minutes in a cool place until required.

2 To make the shortbreads, beat together the butter and caster sugar until light and fluffy, then stir in the flour and ground almonds to make a soft dough. Form this dough into 16 even-sized ovals and place well apart on baking sheets lined with nonstick paper. Press the biscuits lightly with the prongs of a fork.

3 Bake in a preheated oven, 160°C (325°F), Gas Mark 3, for 15 minutes, or until set and lightly coloured. Cool on the baking sheet, then dredge with icing sugar. Serve with the fruit salad and decorate with the remaining sprigs of mint.

I associate sangria with holidays in the sun – and I wanted to turn those flavours into a dessert – hence this recipe.

pink champagne granita marbled with raspberries

berries fizz sugar

serves 4
preparation 15 minutes, plus cooling and freezing
cooking 5 minutes

200 ml (7 fl oz) water
225 g (7½ oz), plus 2 tablespoons caster sugar
1 bottle Pink Champagne
375 g (12 oz) raspberries

1 Put the water into a saucepan with the 225 g (7½ oz) sugar. Heat gently until the sugar has dissolved, then bring to the boil and remove from the heat. Leave to cool.

2 Mix the cooled sugar syrup with the Champagne. Pour into a shallow container so that the mixture is about 1 cm (½ inch) deep and freeze, stirring the mixture from time to time as it becomes frozen around the edges. Because of the alcohol in the Champagne, it will take up to 4 hours to freeze, and will never become rock hard, so can be used straight from the freezer. It's fine to make it the day before needed.

3 To serve, first toss the raspberries in the remaining sugar and set aside for a few minutes until the sugar has dissolved. Put a few raspberries into 4 serving glasses. Give the granita a quick stir with a fork, then scrape some into the glasses, on top of the raspberries. Continue to layer the raspberries and granita into the glasses, then serve immediately.

4 You probably won't need all the granita – it might be called for as second helpings and it makes a wonderful pick-me-up for the cook (or anyone else!) the morning after, perhaps with some freshly squeezed pink grapefruit juice added. Incidentally, ordinary Champagne, rather than pink, is also great to use, but not as pretty.

This recipe makes the most wonderful ending to a special meal.

affogato with almond tuiles

coffee almonds cream

serves 4
preparation 30 minutes
cooking 15–20 minutes

600 ml (1 pint) double or whipping cream
400 g (13 oz) can skimmed condensed milk
150 ml (¼ pint) strong espresso coffee

for the almond tuiles
1 egg white
50 g (2 oz) caster sugar
25 g (1 oz) plain white flour, sifted
25 g (1 oz) butter, melted
40 g (1½ oz) flaked almonds
flavourless vegetable oil such as grapeseed for greasing

1 To make the ice cream, whisk the cream, with an electric whisk for speed and ease, though you can do it by hand, until soft peaks form. Add the condensed milk to the cream and whisk again until combined. Tip into a suitable container – a rigid plastic box is ideal – and freeze until firm.

2 To make the tuiles, whisk the egg white until stiff, then whisk in the sugar. Add the flour and butter alternately to make a smooth mixture. Place big teaspoons of the mixture well apart on a baking sheet lined with nonstick paper (you'll probably get about 4 to a large sheet) and, using the back of the spoon, spread the mixture out to make rounds each about 10 cm (4 inches) in diameter. Sprinkle the top of each with flaked almonds, then bake for 4–5 minutes in a preheated oven, 180°C (350°F), Gas Mark 4, until set and lightly browned, especially around the edges.

3 Remove from the oven and leave to cool for a minute or so until firm enough to lift from the baking sheet. While this is happening, oil a rolling pin. Drape the tuiles over the rolling pin so that as they cool they become curved. Once they're cool they can be removed to a wire rack.

4 Continue with the rest of the mixture to make about 16 tuiles. When they're all cold, store in a tin until needed.

5 To serve, scoop the ice cream into 4 bowls. Pour a couple of tablespoons of the hot coffee over each and serve immediately, with the tuiles.

This is an easy-to-make yet wonderful ice cream. Although freshly brewed espresso is the perfect topping for this – whisper it quietly, instant espresso is also fine: by the time it has mixed with the ice cream, I defy anyone to tell the difference!

white chocolate gelato with citrus drizzle

serves 4
preparation 15 minutes, plus cooling and freezing
cooking 15 minutes

750 ml (1¼ pints) milk
2 x 150 g (5 oz) bars white chocolate, broken into pieces
1½ teaspoons cornflour
125 ml (4 fl oz) double cream

for the citrus drizzle
juice and finely grated rind of 1 orange
juice and finely grated rind of 1 lime
100 g (3½ oz) caster sugar

1 To make the ice cream, put the milk into a saucepan and bring to the boil. Remove from the heat and stir in the chocolate.

2 Put the cornflour in a small bowl with some of the cream and blend to a smooth paste. Reheat the chocolate milk, then tip it into the cornflour mixture, stir and return it to the saucepan, along with the rest of the cream. Bring to the boil, stir for a minute or so until it thickens, then remove from the heat and leave to cool.

3 Pour the cooled mixture into a suitable container for freezing, put into the freezer and leave until solid, stirring from time to time during the freezing process if possible.

4 To make the citrus drizzle, put the orange and lime juices and rinds into a small saucepan with the sugar and gently bring to the boil. Reduce the heat and simmer for about 5 minutes until reduced in quantity and slightly thickened (watch carefully as it burns easily). Set aside until required.

5 To serve, remove the ice cream from the freezer about 30 minutes in advance so that it can soften slightly, then scoop into bowls. Check the citrus drizzle: if it has become very thick, lighten it a bit by stirring in a teaspoon or so of hot water. Then swirl some citrus drizzle over the top of each portion and serve at once.

Because of its light consistency – made mainly with milk rather than cream – gelato takes longer to freeze than normal ice cream and for this reason I find it best to use the freezer rather than an ice-cream maker. Having said that, this gelato couldn't be simpler to make.

chocolate truffles

nuts chocolate cream

makes about 22
preparation 30 minutes, plus chilling
cooking 5 minutes

for the white chocolate and coffee truffles

100 g (3½ oz) white chocolate
25 g (1 oz) cold unsalted butter, cut into small pieces
75 ml (3 fl oz) cold double cream
½ teaspoon instant espresso coffee
1 teaspoon boiling water
100 g (3½ oz) melted white chocolate, sifted cocoa powder or finely ground toasted hazelnuts, to coat

for the milk chocolate truffles with soft centres

100 g (3½ oz) milk chocolate
25 g (1 oz) cold unsalted butter, cut into small pieces
2 tablespoons cold double cream
1 teaspoon brandy (optional)
150 g (5 oz) milk chocolate, sifted cocoa powder or finely ground toasted hazelnuts, to coat

1 To make the white chocolate and coffee truffles, melt the white chocolate in a small bowl set over a pan of gently steaming water. Take the bowl off the heat and stir in first the butter and then the cream. Dissolve the coffee in the boiling water and stir into the mixture, then chill in the refrigerator until firm – about 1 hour.

2 Divide the white chocolate mixture into 10 even-sized pieces and form into balls. Place these on nonstick paper and put into the freezer to chill thoroughly for about 1 hour.

3 To coat with chocolate, dip the frozen chocolates into the melted white chocolate – it will set very quickly – coating both sides. Alternatively, roll the truffles in cocoa powder or finely ground toasted hazelnuts. Put them on nonstick paper and chill in the refrigerator until required.

4 To make the milk chocolate truffles, melt the 100 g (3½ oz) milk chocolate in a small bowl as before, then remove from the heat and beat in the butter, cream and brandy, if you're using this. Chill in the refrigerator until fairly firm, then proceed as described for the white truffles, using milk chocolate, cocoa powder or nuts to coat.

5 Store all the truffles in the refrigerator until required.

These heavenly truffles have rich, creamy centres like Belgian chocolates and are absolutely worth the effort.

alfresco entertaining

I love eating outside: from the first day that's half warm enough to the last of an Indian summer, that's where I'll be … relishing the relaxed food that cries out to be eaten with the fingers, the strong flavours, the informality – and there's a good selection of it in this section.

plantain bhajis with fresh coconut chutney

chilli lime cumin

serves 4 (makes about 20 bhajis)
preparation 20 minutes
cooking 15 minutes

125 g (4 oz) chickpea (gram) flour
½–1 teaspoon dried red chilli flakes
½ teaspoon turmeric
2 teaspoons ground coriander
2 teaspoons ground cumin
2 teaspoons cumin seeds
150–200 ml (5–7 fl oz) sparkling water
1 plantain, about 325 g (11 oz)
rapeseed or groundnut oil for frying
salt, to taste

for the coconut chutney

75 g (3 oz) fresh grated coconut (about ¼ of a coconut)
20 g (¾ oz) packet fresh coriander
juice and grated rind of 1 lime
1 teaspoon black mustard seeds

1 First make the chutney. Put the grated coconut, fresh coriander and lime juice and rind into a food processor and whiz until combined. Stir in the mustard seeds and, if necessary, a little water to make a soft, creamy consistency. Set aside.

2 To make a batter, mix the chickpea flour, chilli flakes, turmeric, ground coriander, ground and whole cumin seeds and some salt with enough sparkling water to make a batter that will coat the back of the spoon.

3 When you are ready to serve the bhajis, heat 2.5 cm (1 inch) of oil in a frying pan. Peel the plantain and cut it diagonally into slices about 2.5 cm (1 inch) thick.

4 Dip a slice of plantain into the batter, then put into the hot oil – it should sizzle immediately. Repeat with several more slices until the frying pan is full. Turn the slices when the underside is golden brown and crisp. When they are done remove them with a slotted spoon on to crumpled kitchen paper. Serve at once in batches, with the chutney – or keep the first ones warm while you fry the rest, then serve all at once, hot and crisp.

courgette and sweetcorn cakes with chilli sauce

garlic dill corn

serves 4
preparation 15 minutes
cooking 15 minutes

2 tablespoons olive oil, plus extra for shallow-frying
250 g (8 oz) baby sweetcorn, sliced into 5 mm (¼ inch) thick rounds
400 g (13 oz) coarsely grated courgette
3 garlic cloves, crushed
5 tablespoons masa harina (see page 184)
1 teaspoon ground cumin
1 teaspoon dried dill weed
salt and pepper, to taste
3 tablespoons chopped coriander
red chilli sauce, to serve

1 Heat the 2 tablespoons of olive oil in a large saucepan, then add the corn, courgette and garlic. Cook gently, stirring often, for about 5 minutes until the vegetables are tender.

2 Add the masa harina, cumin, dill and some salt and pepper and stir well over the heat for 2–3 minutes, until the mixture is very thick and holds together well. Set aside until cool enough to handle, then form into 5 cm (2 inch) diameter cakes. You should make about 12–14.

3 Heat a little olive oil in a frying pan and fry the cakes on both sides until golden brown and crisp. Drain on kitchen paper.

4 Transfer to a serving dish, scatter with the chopped coriander and serve at once with red chilli sauce for dipping.

As these little corncakes hold together so well, you could also cook them on a barbecue instead of frying them.

chickpea and lemon cakes

tahini lemon garlic

serves 4
preparation 20 minutes
cooking 15 minutes

2 x 425 g (14 oz) cans chickpeas
2 garlic cloves, crushed
4 tablespoons freshly squeezed lemon juice
2 tablespoons tahini
salt and pepper, to taste
lemon slices, to garnish

for the coating
6 tablespoons cornflour
5 tablespoons water
25 g (1 oz) dried breadcrumbs
rapeseed or groundnut oil for deep-frying

1 Strain the chickpeas well, reserving the liquid. Put them into a food processor with the garlic, lemon juice, tahini and some salt and pepper and whiz until smooth. If the mixture is fairly stiff, add a little of the reserved chickpea liquid and whiz again. The texture needs to be light and fluffy, but firm enough to be formed into 'cakes'.

2 Put the cornflour into a bowl and mix in the water to make a thick coating paste. Form the chickpea mixture into balls, dip each into the cornflour paste and then into the dried breadcrumbs, turning them to make sure they're thoroughly coated.

3 Heat sufficient oil in a pan for deep-frying to 180–190°C (350–375°F), or until a cube of bread browns in 30 seconds, and fry the cakes for 2–3 minutes. Drain on kitchen paper and serve at once, garnished with lemon slices.

These savoury cakes have all the flavour and creamy texture of hummus within a crisp outer coating.

adzuki, rice and ginger balls with teriyaki dip

beans plums ginger

V

makes 18
preparation 20 minutes
cooking 1 hour 5 minutes

50 g (2 oz) adzuki beans
125 g (4 oz) brown rice
2 teaspoons grated fresh root ginger
300 ml (½ pint) water
2 teaspoons lemon juice
flesh from 2–3 umeboshi plums or 1–2 teaspoons umeboshi paste (see page 185)
2–3 tablespoons sesame seeds
salt and pepper, to taste

for the dip
3 tablespoons shoyu or tamari
3 tablespoons mirin

1 Cover the beans with water and bring to the boil, then reduce the heat, half cover the pan and simmer for 45 minutes, or until tender. Drain.

2 Put the rice and ginger into a saucepan with the measured water. Bring to the boil, then reduce the heat, cover the pan and leave to cook over a very gentle heat for 30–40 minutes, or until the rice is tender and all the water has been absorbed.

3 Put the rice into a food processor with the beans, lemon juice, umeboshi and some salt and pepper and whiz to a thick mixture that holds together.

4 Put the sesame seeds on to a large plate, then break off large marble-sized pieces of the rice mixture and roll them in the seeds to form 18 balls. Place the rice balls on a baking sheet and bake in a preheated oven, 180°C (350°F), Gas Mark 4, for 20 minutes, or until crisp on the outside.

5 To make the dip, mix the shoyu or tamari with the mirin in a small bowl and serve with the rice balls.

aubergine steaks with mint glaze

lime honey mint

V

serves 4
preparation 10 minutes, plus marinating
cooking 20 minutes

2 large aubergines, stems trimmed
juice of 1 lime
2 tablespoons toasted sesame oil
2 tablespoons clear honey or maple syrup
4 tablespoons chopped mint

1 Cut each aubergine lengthways into 4 thick slices. Cut cross-hatching on both surfaces of the slices – on two of them you will be cutting the skin. Place the aubergine slices on a shallow tray or grill pan.

2 Mix the lime juice with the sesame oil and honey or maple syrup. Drizzle this over the surfaces of the aubergine, turning them over to drench both sides. Leave to marinate for 30 minutes, or up to 8 hours.

3 Grill the aubergine slices under a hot grill or over a barbecue until browned on one side, then turn over to grill the other side until both sides are tender and lightly browned – about 20 minutes.

4 Scatter with the chopped mint and serve at once.

So simple – and so delicious – this has become one of my favourite ways to cook aubergine.

spice-crusted tofu with maple glaze

nuts tofu syrup

serves 4
preparation 10 minutes
cooking 10 minutes

3 tablespoons paprika
3 teaspoons ground cumin
3 teaspoons ground coriander
1½ teaspoons salt
3 x 250 g (8 oz) blocks firm tofu, drained
6 tablespoons olive oil
9 tablespoons boiling water
6 tablespoons freshly squeezed lemon juice
4½ tablespoons maple syrup
50 g (2 oz) pine nuts, toasted
pepper, to taste

1 Mix the paprika with the ground cumin and coriander, the salt and a grinding of black pepper and spread out on a plate.

2 Cut the tofu blocks in half, then slice each half horizontally to make 4 'steaks'. Dip the tofu in the spices, coating all sides.

3 Heat the olive oil in a frying pan, add the tofu and cook until brown and crusty on one side, 4–5 minutes, then turn the pieces over and cook the other side.

4 While the tofu is cooking, mix the boiling water with the lemon juice and maple syrup. Add this mixture to the pan – it will bubble up and disappear very quickly, leaving a sticky glaze.

5 Transfer the tofu to a serving dish, sprinkle with the pine nuts and serve immediately.

chunky smoked cheese and parsley sausages

shallots parsley

makes 12
preparation 10 minutes
cooking 5–10 minutes

2 x 150 g (5 oz) packets Bavarian smoked cheese, grated
175 g (6 oz) soft wholemeal breadcrumbs
6 tablespoons chopped parsley
2 shallots
olive oil for shallow-frying or brushing
salt and pepper, to taste
hot pepper sauce, to serve

1 Put the grated cheese, breadcrumbs, parsley, shallots and a little salt and pepper into a food processor and whiz to a smooth mixture that holds together. Form into 12 fat chunky sausages.

2 Shallow-fry the sausages in a little hot olive oil for 5 minutes, or brush all over with olive oil and cook on a barbecue, turning them so that they become crisp and golden brown all over.

3 Serve at once with hot pepper sauce, while they are hot and crisp on the outside, melting and tender within.

dough ball, halloumi and olive skewers

butter cheese lemons

serves 4
preparation 20 minutes, plus rising
cooking 10–15 minutes

2 x 250 g (8 oz) blocks halloumi cheese, drained
24 large green olives, pitted
olive oil for brushing

for the dough balls
250 g (8 oz) strong white bread flour
½ packet fast-action dried yeast
1 teaspoon salt
175 ml (6 fl oz) warm water
2 tablespoons olive oil

for the lemon butter
juice and grated rind of ½ lemon
125 g (4 oz) soft butter

1 To make the dough balls, put the flour into a food processor fitted with a plastic dough blade. Add the yeast, salt, water and olive oil and pulse until a dough forms, then blend for 1 minute. Leave, with the lid on, for 45 minutes, or until the dough has doubled in size.

2 Divide the dough into 24 equal pieces and roll into marble-sized balls.

3 Cut each block of halloumi into 12 cubes. Thread a dough ball on to a skewer followed by an olive and a cube of halloumi; repeat twice so that each skewer contains 3 dough balls, pieces of cheese and olives. Brush lightly with olive oil and place on a grill pan or baking sheet. When all the skewers are done, cover them with a piece of polythene or a clean damp cloth and leave for 50–60 minutes for the dough balls to rise.

4 These skewers can be cooked in the oven, at 200°C (400°F), Gas Mark 6, under the grill, or on a barbecue: preheat these in advance, then cook the skewers, turning them when the first side is done. They will take about 5 minutes on each side.

5 To make the lemon butter, beat the lemon juice and rind into the softened butter and serve with the dough ball skewers.

The dough balls are quick and easy to make, but, if you prefer, use shop-bought frozen dough balls, thawed. You need 8 skewers for this recipe – if you use wooden ones soak them in cold water for 10 minutes before use to prevent them burning.

mexican tart with cumin pastry

eggs peppers chilli

serves 4
preparation 30 minutes
cooking 1 hour

2 onions, chopped
2 green peppers, cored, deseeded and chopped
1 tablespoon olive oil
2 x 400 g (13 oz) cans chopped tomatoes
½ teaspoon dried red chilli flakes
5 very fresh eggs
salt and pepper, to taste

for the cumin pastry
250 g (8 oz) plain flour
2 teaspoons cumin seeds
125 g (4 oz) butter
about 4 tablespoons cold water

1 To make the cumin pastry, put the flour and cumin seeds into a bowl, add the butter and rub in with your fingertips until the mixture resembles fine breadcrumbs. Add enough cold water – 3–4 tablespoons – to mix to a malleable dough. Turn the dough out on to a lightly floured surface and knead briefly. Roll out to fit a deep greased 30 cm (12 inch) flan tin, ease the pastry into place, then press down and trim the edges. Prick the base, then cover it with nonstick paper and some dried beans to weigh the pastry down.

2 Bake the flan case in a preheated oven, 200°C (400°F), Gas Mark 6, for 20 minutes, until set and crisp. Remove the paper and beans and bake the flan case for a further 10 minutes until the base is crisp. Remove the case from the oven and reduce the oven temperature to 180°C (350°F), Gas Mark 4.

3 Meanwhile, make the filling. Fry the onions and green peppers in the olive oil, covered, for 5 minutes, until beginning to get tender, then add the tomatoes and chilli flakes and simmer, uncovered, over a moderate heat for 25–30 minutes, or until very thick, stirring from time to time to prevent sticking. Remove from the heat and season with salt and pepper.

4 Spoon the tomato filling evenly into the pastry case. Make a depression in the centre, for one of the eggs, and four more evenly spaced around the edge. Break the eggs into the depressions and season lightly.

5 Cover the flan with foil, return to the oven and bake for about 20 minutes, or until the eggs are set.

This dramatic-looking tart has a hot and spicy red filling topped with eggs. To help the eggs set neatly, use very fresh eggs taken straight from the refrigerator.

potato and white truffle torte

butter garlic parsley

serves 4
preparation 20 minutes
cooking 30 minutes

1 kg (2 lb) potatoes, peeled and cut into 5 mm (¼ inch) thick slices
2 garlic cloves, crushed
40 g (1½ oz) butter
50 g (2 oz) white truffle, wiped, or 80 g (3¼ oz) jar porcini mushrooms in a vegetarian white truffle paste (see page 184)
200 g (7 oz) Parmesan-style cheese, grated
salt and pepper, to taste
flat leaf parsley, to garnish

1 Cook the potatoes in boiling water to cover for about 10 minutes, or until tender but not soft. Drain.

2 Mix the garlic into the butter and use half to grease generously a 23–25 cm (9–10 inch) springform tin. Arrange a layer of potato in the tin, then grate some of the truffle over the top, or spread some truffle paste over the potatoes. Sprinkle with cheese and season with salt and pepper.

3 Continue these layers, seasoning with salt and pepper between each layer, until you have used all the ingredients, ending with a layer of potato and one of cheese. Dot with the remaining butter.

4 Bake in a preheated oven, 230°C (450°F), Gas Mark 8, for about 20 minutes, or until golden brown and crisp on top.

5 Remove the sides of the tin, slide the torte (on its base) on to a warmed plate, snip some parsley over the top and serve at once.

This has a wonderful rich and seductive flavour. White truffle is fantastic in this if available, but you can also make a very good version using Porcini and White Truffle Paste. It's very rich: great with a refreshing green salad.

cavalo nero and goats' cheese torte

raisins nuts cheese

serves 4
preparation 20 minutes
cooking 25 minutes

425 g (14 oz) bunch of cavalo nero, tough stems removed, leaves shredded
2 x 100 g (3½ oz) packets soft goats' cheese, cut into rough chunks
40 g (1½ oz) raisins
375 g (12 oz) frozen ready-rolled all-butter puff pastry (see page 184)
25 g (1 oz) pine nuts
25 g (1 oz) Pecorino, or other hard Italian Parmesan-style cheese, grated
salt and pepper, to taste

1 Cook the cavalo nero in 2.5 cm (1 inch) of boiling water for 7–10 minutes, or until tender. Drain very well and leave to cool.

2 Add the goats' cheese and raisins to the cavalo nero, along with some salt and pepper, and mix gently but thoroughly.

3 Roll the pastry a little more, then cut out a circle about 33 cm (13 inches) in diameter. Lay the pastry circle on a baking sheet.

4 Spoon the cavolo nero mixture on to the pastry circle, leaving about 2.5 cm (1 inch) clear all around the edges and smoothing it level. Then fold up the edges and press them together to make a crust. Sprinkle the top with pine nuts and grated cheese. Cut some long strips from the remaining pastry and make a lattice over the top of the filling.

5 Bake the torte in a preheated oven, 200°C (400°F), Gas Mark 6, for about 15 minutes, or until it is puffed up and golden brown on top. Eat the torte hot, warm or cold.

mimosa egg salad with tarragon

eggs lettuce mayo

serves 4
preparation 10 minutes
cooking 10 minutes

8 eggs, hardboiled
4 tablespoons mayonnaise
20 g (¾ oz) fresh tarragon, chopped
8 crisp, cup-shaped lettuce leaves from an ordinary round-head or iceberg lettuce
salt and pepper, to taste

1 Separate the egg whites from the yolks and chop both finely.

2 Mix the egg whites and all but 1 tablespoon of the yolks with the mayonnaise and most of the chopped tarragon. Season with salt and pepper.

3 Arrange the lettuce leaves in a single layer in a shallow serving dish. Spoon the egg mixture loosely into each lettuce leaf – it doesn't have to be too neat and tidy – then scatter the remaining chopped egg yolk and tarragon over the top and serve.

Very pretty and refreshing, this is great as an accompaniment or, on individual plates, as a starter.

jamaican jerk sweet potato

spices lime chives

serves 4
preparation 20 minutes
cooking 20 minutes

4 sweet potatoes, about 350 g (11½ oz) each
lime wedges, to serve (optional)

for the jerk spice paste
1 onion, roughly chopped
1 red chilli, deseeded
4 garlic cloves
4 teaspoons dried thyme
2 teaspoons allspice
1 teaspoon ground cinnamon
½ teaspoon ground nutmeg
2 tablespoons olive oil
1 teaspoon salt
1 teaspoon pepper

for the chive yogurt
2 tablespoons chopped chives
300 g (10 oz) natural yogurt
salt and pepper, to taste

1 To make the jerk paste, put all the ingredients into a food processor and whiz to a paste.

2 Cut the sweet potatoes into wedges about 5 mm (¼ inch) thick – they need to be thin enough to cook through without burning. Spread the cut surfaces of the wedges with the jerk paste and place under a hot grill or on a barbecue grid. Cook for 5 minutes on each side, or until the sweet potato is tender to the point of a knife and the jerk paste is crunchy and slightly charred.

3 Stir the chives into the yogurt along with some salt and pepper and put into a small bowl.

4 Serve the sweet potato wedges at once while still sizzling hot, accompanied by the chive yogurt, wedges of lime and plenty of soft bread, if liked.

It's easy to make your own jerk paste, but for a very fast option, use a shop-bought one instead.

leek rice with almonds and red pepper mayo

rice olives peppers

serves 4
preparation 20 minutes
cooking 20–25 minutes

250 g (8 oz) white basmati rice
1 teaspoon turmeric
450 ml (¾ pint) water
450 g (14½ oz) leeks, cut into 2.5 cm (1 inch) pieces
2 tablespoons freshly squeezed lemon juice
1 tablespoon olive oil
2 teaspoons black mustard seeds
4 tablespoons toasted flaked almonds
50 g (2 oz) small green olives
salt and pepper, to taste

for the red pepper mayo

1 large red pepper, halved, cored and deseeded
2 tablespoons red wine vinegar
6 tablespoons olive oil
2 teaspoons caster sugar

1 Put the rice into a saucepan with the turmeric and water. Bring to the boil, then turn the heat down as low as possible, cover the pan and leave to cook for about 10 minutes. Remove from the heat without removing the lid and leave to stand for 5–10 minutes.

2 Meanwhile, cook the leeks in boiling water to cover for about 10 minutes, or until tender. Drain.

3 Add the lemon juice to the rice along with some salt and pepper, stirring gently, then mix the leeks into the rice.

4 Heat the olive oil in a small pan, add the mustard seeds and fry for 1–2 minutes, or until they're sizzling. Add to the leek mixture, along with the flaked almonds and olives.

5 To make the mayo, put the red pepper halves cut-side down on a grill pan and cook under a hot grill for about 10 minutes, or until black and blistered in places. Cool, then strip off the skin. Blend the peppers with the wine vinegar, olive oil, sugar and some salt and pepper in a food processor, blender or using a stick blender, to make a smooth, thick, brick-red sauce. Serve with the rice. This dish can be served hot, warm or cold.

buckwheat and mango tabbouleh

mango mint lime

serves 4
preparation 10 minutes, plus standing
cooking 3–4 minutes

250 g (8 oz) raw buckwheat
1 large ripe juicy mango
bunch of mint, chopped
juice of 1 lime
salt and pepper, to taste

1 Put the buckwheat into a dry saucepan and stir over a moderate heat for 3–4 minutes, or until the buckwheat smells toasty and is turning light golden brown. Remove from the heat, cover with boiling water and set aside for 10–15 minutes to soften.

2 Cut the mango down each side of the stone. Remove all the skin, slice the flesh and put into a bowl.

3 When the buckwheat has softened – when you can squash a grain between your finger and thumb – drain it and put into a bowl. Stir in the mango, mint, lime juice and some salt and pepper. Eat at once or store in a cool place for a few hours.

You can buy buckwheat at organic and healthfood shops. Be sure to get the raw, untoasted type.

green olives with mixed peppercorns and coriander

oil garlic olives

serves 4
preparation 10 minutes, plus marinating

340 g (11½ oz) can green queen olives in brine, drained
2 garlic cloves, finely sliced
1 lemon
1 tablespoon coriander seeds
1 tablespoon mixed peppercorns – black, white, green, pink and pimiento
extra virgin olive oil for marinating

1 Put the olives into a bowl with the garlic. Cut thin strips of rind from half the lemon, using a zester if possible, and add to the olives. Slice the remaining half of the lemon thinly, then cut the slices into smaller pieces again and add to the bowl.

2 Crush the coriander seeds and peppercorns coarsely using a pestle and mortar or by putting them into a strong polythene bag and bashing with a rolling pin. Add to the bowl, then pour in enough olive oil to cover the olives and leave to marinate for at least 1 hour, or longer if there's time.

Why marinate your own olives when you can buy them? Because they're so easy to make yourself and you can rustle them up when you want them from storecupboard ingredients – but most of all, because these are divine!

butterbean salad with sweet chilli dressing

beans celery onion

V

serves 4
preparation 5 minutes

2 x 420 g (14 oz) cans butterbeans, drained and rinsed
1 teaspoon dried crushed red peppers
2 teaspoons maple syrup
2 tablespoons rice vinegar
2 teaspoons toasted sesame oil
2 teaspoons shoyu or tamari
2 spring onions, thinly sliced
3–4 tablespoons roughly chopped celery leaves
50 g (2 oz) salted peanuts, crushed
pepper, to taste

1 Put the butterbeans into a bowl, add the crushed red peppers, maple syrup, rice vinegar, sesame oil, shoyu or tamari and a grinding of pepper and stir gently to mix.

2 Add the spring onions and celery leaves, then stir again. Add the crushed peanuts just before serving, so that they remain crisp.

quick yeasted herb and garlic flat bread

thyme salt yeast

V

serves 4
preparation 20 minutes, plus rising
cooking 20–30 minutes

500 g (1 lb) strong white bread flour
1 packet fast-action dried yeast
2 teaspoons sea salt plus extra for sprinkling
350 ml (12 fl oz) warm water
6 tablespoons olive oil
4 tablespoons chopped thyme

1 Put the flour into a food processor fitted with a plastic dough blade. Add the yeast, the 2 teaspoons of salt, the water and 2 tablespoons of the olive oil and pulse until a dough forms, then blend for 1 minute. Leave, with the lid on, for 45 minutes, or until the dough has doubled in size.

2 Add the chopped thyme and process briefly to mix, then remove the dough from the machine, divide in half and press each into a wide 900 g (1 lb 13 oz) loaf tin or 20 cm (8 inch) square tin. Cover with clingfilm and leave for 1 hour to rise.

3 Press your fingers into the top of the bread a few times and drizzle the rest of the olive oil over the loaves and into the holes, then sprinkle with some sea salt.

4 Bake the loaves in a preheated oven, 200°C (400°F), Gas Mark 6, for 20–30 minutes, or until the loaves are golden brown on top and sound hollow when turned out of the tins and tapped on the base. (The timing will depend on the exact size of your tin – the deeper the dough in the tin, the longer it will take to cook.)

5 Cool on a wire rack, or wrap each loaf in a clean tea cloth and allow to cool slowly if you want the bread to have a soft crust.

This is a very easy bread that you both mix and let rise in the food processor! It couldn't be simpler.

honey corn muffins

seeds eggs honey

makes 12
preparation 20 minutes
cooking 10–15 minutes

75 g (3 oz) wholemeal flour
100 g (3½ oz) coarse cornmeal or polenta
2½ teaspoons baking powder
30 g (1¼ oz) sunflower seeds
2 eggs
175 ml (6 fl oz) milk
6 tablespoons clear honey
2 tablespoons olive oil

1 Line a muffin tin with 12 paper cases.

2 Put the flour into a bowl with the cornmeal or polenta, the baking powder and half the sunflower seeds.

3 Whisk together the eggs, milk, honey and olive oil, then stir quickly into the dry ingredients – don't mix it too much.

4 Divide the mixture between the paper cases and sprinkle the remaining sunflower seeds on top of each muffin. Bake in a preheated oven, 200°C (400°F), Gas Mark 6, for 10–15 minutes until risen, golden and firm to a light touch. These muffins are delicious for breakfast straight from the oven, or can be reheated for a few minutes before serving.

fruit fajita pudding

pears coconut grapes

serves 4
preparation 25 minutes
cooking 15 minutes

for the fajitas
125 g (4 oz) plain white flour
2 teaspoons caster sugar
2 eggs
300 ml (½ pint) milk and water mixed
a little flavourless oil, such as groundnut, for shallow-frying

for the fruit salad
2 ripe pears, peeled and cut into bite-sized pieces
125 g (4 oz) small strawberries, hulled
125 g (4 oz) purple or red seedless grapes, halved
2 ripe kiwi fruit, peeled and sliced
juice of 1 orange

to serve
toasted almonds or coconut
whipped double cream
maple syrup
caster sugar
slices of lime

1 All the preparation for this can be done in advance. First make the fajitas, which are in fact sweet pancakes. Put the flour, sugar, eggs and most of the milk and water into a blender or food processor and blend to a smooth batter, adding the rest of the liquid if necessary to make a consistency like single cream. Alternatively, sift the flour into a bowl, add the sugar and break in the eggs. Beat together, adding the liquid gradually to make a smooth batter.

2 Heat 1 tablespoon of oil in a frying pan. When it's hot, swirl the oil around the pan and tip any excess into a cup. Pour in a good 2 tablespoons of the batter and tip the pan so that it spreads all over the base – you may need a bit more or less batter, depending on the size of your frying pan, but the pancakes need to be thick enough to be rolled around the fruit salad filling later – more robust than delicate crêpes!

3 After a minute or so, when the top of the pancake has set, flip it over with a palette knife to cook the other side, which will take only a few seconds. Put the pancake on to a plate and continue to make more in the same way, piling them up on the plate. Grease the frying pan with more oil as required.

4 Make the fruit salad by mixing all the fruits together and adding the orange juice. Put into a serving bowl and keep cool.

5 Serve a pile of fajitas with the bowl of fruit salad and small bowls of toasted almonds or coconut, whipped double cream, maple syrup, caster sugar and lime slices, for people to help themselves. Plenty of napkins and finger bowls might be a good idea.

This sweet version of fajitas makes a fun help-yourself pudding, ideal for an informal meal with friends.

party time

Party time is show-off time – and here are some stunning recipes. Some are tiny – 'just a mouthful' – but none are difficult. Some can be served cold, others made and reheated or cooked at the last minute. Serve 3–4 different types; each type on its own platter; and allow 5–7 nibbles per person.

canapés: bruschette with three toppings

tahini garlic oil

makes 24
preparation 40 minutes
cooking 30 minutes

1 rosemary loaf, or 1 baguette and dried rosemary
olive oil
salt and pepper, to taste

for the aubergine caviar
2 aubergines
1–2 garlic cloves, crushed
2 tablespoons tahini
2 tablespoons olive oil plus extra to garnish
2 tablespoons freshly squeezed lemon juice
garlic sprouts, to garnish (optional)

for the goats' cheese with red onion and beetroot
450 g (14½ oz) red onions, thinly sliced
1 tablespoon olive oil
1 tablespoon caster sugar
1 tablespoon red wine vinegar
450 g (14½ oz) cooked beetroot, diced
200 g (7 oz) soft goats' cheese
rosemary leaves, to garnish

for the chestnut pâté
200 g (7 oz) vacuum pack whole peeled chestnuts
15 g (½ oz) butter
1 garlic clove, crushed
2 tablespoons freshly squeezed lemon juice
paprika pepper (or finely chopped small sweet red peppers from a jar) and sprigs of thyme, to garnish

1 Start by making the bruschette. Slice the bread, then brush each slice on both sides with olive oil. If you're using a plain baguette, sprinkle each piece on both sides with a good pinch of crushed rosemary. Place the bread on a baking sheet and bake in a preheated oven, 150°C (300°F), Gas Mark 2, for about 20 minutes until crisp. Cool on wire racks. They can be made up to 1 week in advance and kept in an airtight container.

2 Next make the fillings. For the aubergine caviar, prick the aubergines in several places, then cook them under a very hot grill for 25–30 minutes until soft and well charred. Cool slightly, then peel off the skin and whiz the aubergine to a pale cream with the garlic, tahini, the 2 tablespoons of olive oil and the lemon juice. Season with salt and pepper and chill until required.

3 For the caramelized onion and beetroot, cook the onions in the olive oil in a large saucepan, covered, for about 15 minutes until they're very tender, stirring them every 5 minutes. Add the sugar, wine vinegar and beetroot, then simmer gently, uncovered, for 10–15 minutes. Remove from the heat, season and cool.

4 For the chestnut pâté, put the chestnuts into a food processor with the butter, garlic and lemon juice. Whiz to a fairly smooth purée and season with salt and pepper.

5 To prepare the bruschette, spread one-third of the bases with aubergine caviar and garnish with a drizzle of olive oil and a few garlic sprouts, if liked. Spread another third of the bases with goats' cheese, top with caramelized onion and beetroot and a piece of rosemary. Spread the remaining bruschette with chestnut pâté and garnish with a dusting of paprika pepper or sweet red peppers and thyme sprigs.

mini carrot and cardamom tarte tatins

carrots oil pastry

makes 16
preparation 25 minutes
cooking 35 minutes

750 g (1½ lb) carrots, very thinly sliced
1 large garlic clove, crushed
3 tablespoons olive oil
175 ml (6 fl oz) water
1½ teaspoons caster sugar
20 cardamom pods
375 g (12 oz) frozen ready-rolled all-butter puff pastry (see page 184)
salt and pepper, to taste

1 Put the carrots into a saucepan with the garlic, olive oil, water, sugar and some salt and pepper.

2 Crush the cardamom and discard the pods. Crush the seeds a little, then add to the saucepan. Bring to the boil, then reduce the heat, cover the pan and cook gently for about 10 minutes, or until the carrots are tender and glossy, and the water has disappeared. If there is still water left, remove the lid of the pan and boil the liquid rapidly until it has disappeared. Cool.

3 Line a 22 x 32 cm (8½ x 12½ inch) Swiss roll tin with nonstick paper. Spread the carrots evenly over the bottom and cover with the pastry, pressing it down and trimming it to fit. Prick the pastry all over, then bake in a preheated oven, 200°C (400°F), Gas Mark 6, for 15 minutes until puffy, golden brown and crisp.

4 Leave the tart to cool completely, then turn it out on to a board so that the carrot is on top. Using a sharp round cutter, 3.5 cm (1½ inches) in diameter, carefully cut out 16 circles. You may need to use a sharp knife in addition to the cutter to get through the pastry.

5 Just before serving, put the little tarte tatins on to an ovenproof serving dish and pop them into the oven for a few minutes to warm through.

With their crisp flaky pastry bases and glossy orange tops of tender, melting carrot, these are gorgeous and not difficult to make.

mini watercress roulade slices

eggs watercress cheese

makes 18
preparation 25 minutes
cooking 12–15 minutes

25 g (1 oz) butter
2 x 75 g (3 oz) packets watercress, finely chopped
3 eggs
150 g (5 oz) garlic and herb cream cheese
salt and pepper, to taste

1 Melt the butter in a saucepan, add the watercress and cook over a moderate heat for about 3 minutes, or until the watercress has wilted.

2 Purée the watercress in a food processor, then add the eggs and some salt and pepper and whiz until combined.

3 Line a 22 x 32 cm (8½ x 12½ inch) Swiss roll tin with a piece of nonstick paper and pour the mixture in, making sure it flows into the corners. Bake in a preheated oven, 200°C (400°F), Gas Mark 6, for about 12 minutes, or until set. Remove from the oven and leave to cool.

4 Turn the roulade out on to a piece of nonstick paper and strip off the backing paper.

5 Beat the cream cheese in a bowl until soft, adding 1–2 tablespoons of hot water if necessary, then spread evenly over the top of the roulade.

6 With the long side facing you, make an incision about 5 mm (¼ inch) in from the edge, but don't cut right through. Bend this piece of roulade up, pressing it against the filling, then continue to roll it firmly to make a small Swiss roll. Wrap in nonstick paper until required, then unwrap and cut into 18 little slices to serve.

These are really very easy to do, and look and taste impressive.

oriental omelette wraps

radish mirin sesame

makes 20
preparation 30 minutes
cooking 15 minutes

10 cm (4 inch) piece of cucumber, peeled
4 spring onions
1 tablespoon rice vinegar
1 tablespoon shoyu or tamari
1 tablespoon mirin
4 eggs
toasted sesame oil
salt and pepper, to taste

to garnish
sesame seeds
radish roses
spring onion tassels

1 Cut the cucumber and spring onions into matchsticks about 5 cm (2 inches) long. Put them into a shallow dish and add the rice vinegar, shoyu or tamari and the mirin, then mix gently and set aside.

2 Beat the eggs with some salt and pepper. Coat a frying pan thinly with sesame oil and heat.

3 Pour about 1 tablespoon of the beaten egg into the frying pan. Let it run a little, but tilt the frying pan so that the omelette stays as round as possible. When the top has set completely, lift the omelette from the pan with a fish slice, roll it up lightly, put it on a plate and continue making another 19 omelettes in the same way, until all the egg has been used.

4 Unroll one of the omelettes, put a few matchsticks of cucumber and one of spring onion in the centre and re-roll it. Place on a serving dish, seam side down. Make the rest in the same way, arranging them all around the edge of a plate, like the spokes of a wheel.

5 Sprinkle with a few sesame seeds and put some radish roses and spring onion tassels in the centre of the plate to garnish. Keep cool until required.

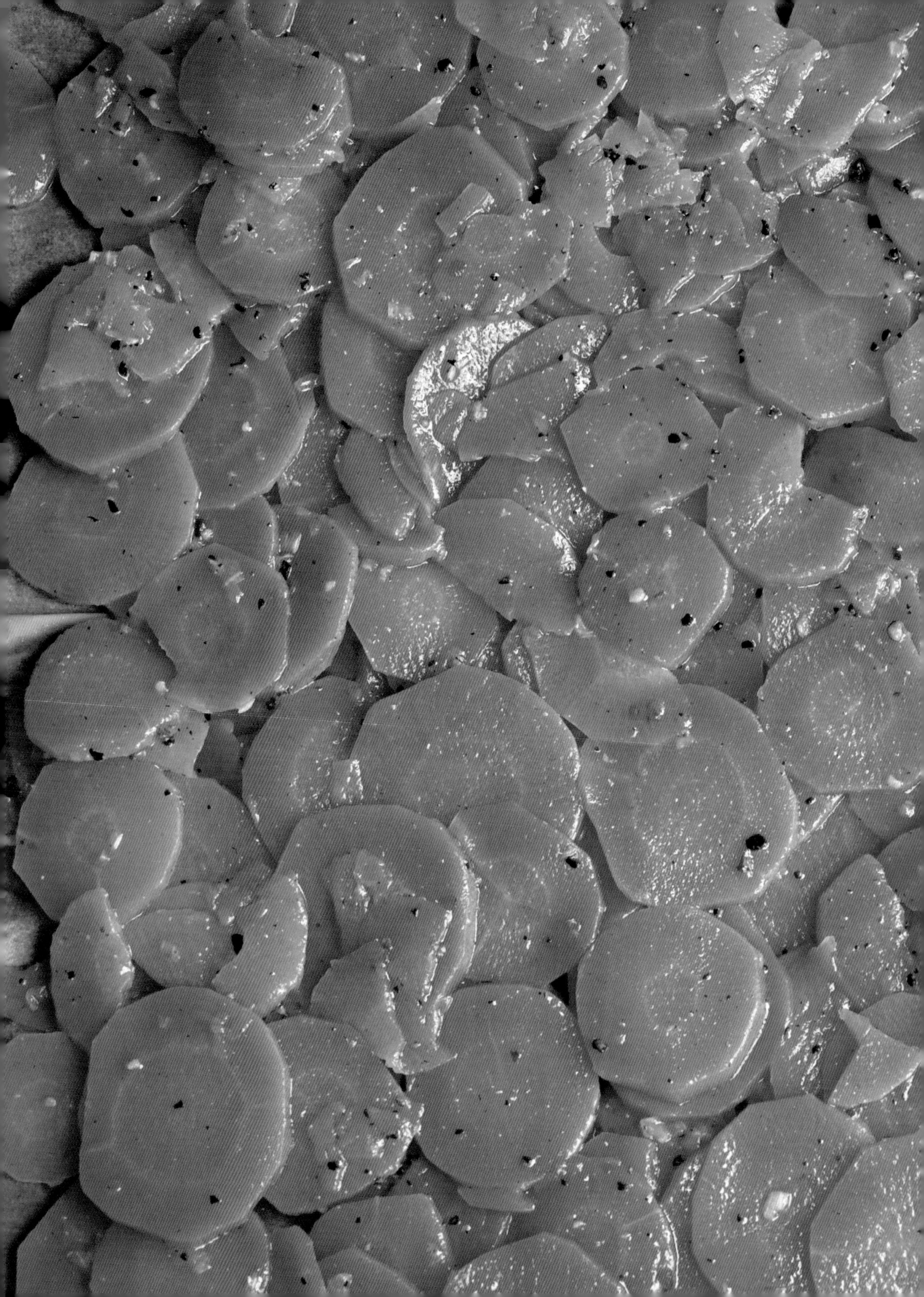

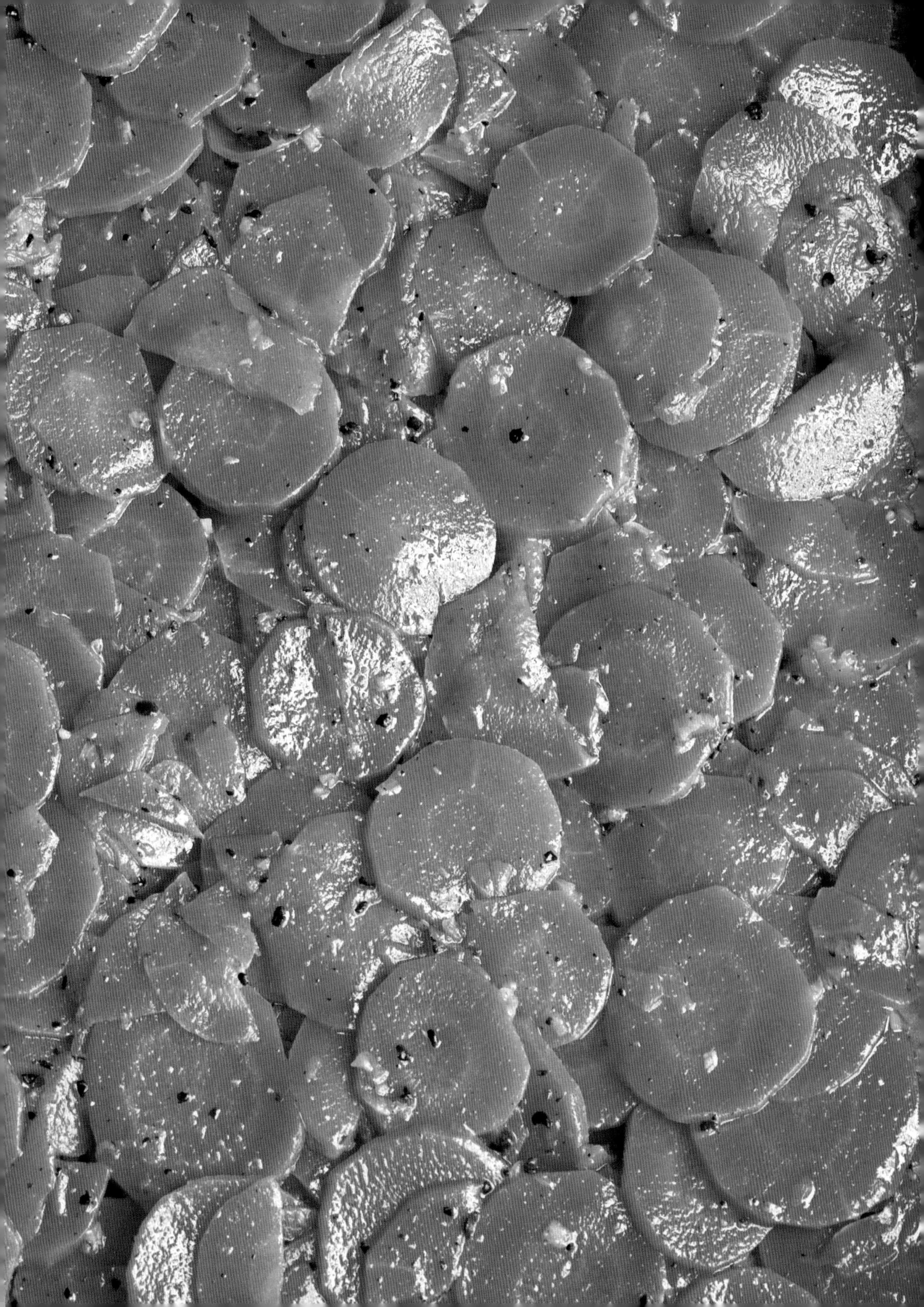

tiny tortillas

chives cheese cream

makes 20
preparation 15 minutes
cooking 30 minutes

500 g (1 lb) potatoes, peeled and cut into even-sized pieces
4 spring onions, chopped
1 red pepper, cored, deseeded and very finely chopped
2 eggs, beaten
olive oil for frying
50 g (2 oz) grated Gruyère cheese
5–6 cherry tomatoes, sliced
salt and pepper, to taste
150 ml (¼ pint) soured cream and 2 tablespoons chopped chives, to garnish (optional)

1 Cover the potatoes in boiling water and cook for about 10 minutes until they are just tender. Drain and cool.

2 Cut the potatoes into small cubes – about 2.5 cm (1 inch) – then mix with the spring onions, red pepper, eggs and some salt and pepper.

3 Heat a little olive oil in a frying pan. Put heaped dessertspoons of the tortilla mixture into the hot oil, forming them into circles, and cook gently for about 5 minutes, or until the bases of the tortillas are golden brown and the tops have more or less set. Remove from the frying pan on to a plate lined with kitchen paper and keep cool until you want to serve them.

4 Place the tortillas, in a single layer, on a flat ovenproof plate. Top each tortilla with a little Gruyère and a slice of tomato, then pop them under a hot grill or into a hot oven for about 5 minutes, or until they are heated through and the tops are golden brown. Garnish each with a teaspoon of soured cream and some chopped chives, if liked, and serve at once.

These are delectable as they are, garnished with a spoonful of chive soured cream, or served with a bowl of soured cream and chives for dipping.

mini feta and sun-dried tomato muffins

basil feta tomato

makes 30
preparation 10 minutes
cooking 10 minutes

- 2 tablespoons olive oil plus extra for greasing
- 1 egg
- 2 tablespoons sun-dried tomato paste
- 2 tablespoons water
- 125 g (4 oz) plain white flour
- 2 teaspoons baking powder
- 200 g (7 oz) feta cheese, cut into tiny dice
- 8 sun-dried tomatoes in oil, drained and finely chopped
- 4 tablespoons lightly chopped basil
- salt and pepper, to taste

1 Line the bases of a 12-hole mini-muffin tin, each hole measuring 1.5 cm (¾ inch) across and about 1.5 cm (¾ inch) deep, with circles of nonstick paper, then brush them with olive oil. Or line them with mini paper cases if you have them.

2 Beat together the rest of the olive oil, the egg, tomato paste and water.

3 Sift together the flour and baking powder into a bowl, then mix in the feta, sun-dried tomatoes, basil and some salt and pepper. Make a well in the centre and add the egg mixture. Stir until just combined – do not over mix.

4 Spoon into the mini-muffin tin holes or cases, filling them well, and bake in a preheated oven, 190°C (375°F), Gas Mark 5, for about 8 minutes, or until golden brown.

5 Remove from the oven and leave for 5 minutes to settle, then slip them out of the tin with a knife and leave to cool on a wire rack.

6 The muffins can be reheated before serving: put them on an ovenproof plate and pop them into a preheated moderate oven, 180°C (350°F), Gas Mark 4, for about 5 minutes, to heat through and puff up.

If you use non-stick mini-muffin tins it's easy to get the muffins out – or, even easier, you could line them with mini paper cake cases ('bonbon' cases) which look attractive, too.

pecorino bites

egg truffle cheese

makes 12
preparation 20 minutes
cooking 20 minutes

450 g (14½ oz) potatoes, peeled and cut into even-sized pieces
2 tablespoons truffle oil
25 g (1 oz) Pecorino cheese, grated
1–2 teaspoons porcini mushrooms in a vegetarian white truffle paste (see page 184)
1 large egg, beaten
4–6 tablespoons dried breadcrumbs
rapeseed or groundnut oil for deep-frying
salt and pepper, to taste

1 Cover the potatoes in boiling water and cook for about 15 minutes, or until tender. Drain thoroughly. Mash the potatoes with the truffle oil, Pecorino and some salt and pepper. Set aside until cool enough to handle.

2 Divide the mixture into 12 equal portions. Flatten each piece, then put a small spoonful – about ⅛ of a teaspoon – of truffle paste on to the centre of each. Take each of the rounds, draw the sides up so that the truffle paste is enclosed, and form into a ball shape. Dip the balls first in beaten egg and then in dried breadcrumbs, so that they are completely coated.

3 Heat sufficient oil for deep-frying to 180–190°C (350–375°F), or until a cube of bread browns in 30 seconds, and fry the potato balls for 2–3 minutes, or until golden and crisp. Drain on kitchen paper. Serve hot, warm or cold.

smoked tofu mini-skewers with satay dip

basil ginger chilli

makes 32
preparation 20 minutes
cooking 20–30 minutes

2 x 220 g (7½ oz) blocks smoked tofu, drained
1–2 tablespoons toasted sesame oil
small bunch of Thai basil or fresh coriander

for the satay dip
1 tablespoon unsweetened peanut butter, smooth or chunky
½ teaspoon grated fresh root ginger
1 garlic clove, crushed to a paste
½ x 400 g (13 oz) can organic coconut milk
dried red chilli flakes
salt and pepper, to taste
mild paprika pepper, to garnish

1 Cut each block of tofu into 4 fingers, then cut each of these into 4, to make 16 cubes. Toss the cubes in the sesame oil, put on to a grill pan and cook under a medium-hot grill until brown and crisp all over, turning them to cook each side of the cubes. This process will take 20–30 minutes. Don't rush it – it's important to get the tofu nice and crisp.

2 Meanwhile, make the satay dip. Put the peanut butter, ginger and garlic into a bowl and mix, then gradually stir in the coconut milk to make a smooth, thick sauce. Add a pinch or two of chilli flakes, to give it a bit of a kick, and some salt and pepper. Put into a small serving bowl and set aside.

3 Put a small Thai basil or coriander leaf and a cube of tofu on to each of 32 cocktail sticks. Put the bowl of dip on a serving plate and sprinkle with a little paprika. Arrange the tofu mini-skewers around the bowl of dip and serve. The tofu can be served hot or cold.

baby yorkshire puddings with nut roast and horseradish

herbs almonds soy

makes 24
preparation 20 minutes, plus standing
cooking 35 minutes

50 g (2 oz) plain white flour
1 egg
75 ml (3 fl oz) milk
75 ml (3 fl oz) water
2 tablespoons olive oil plus extra for greasing
salt and pepper, to taste
horseradish sauce, to serve

for the nut roast
50 g (2 oz) almonds
25 g (1 oz) wholemeal bread
50 g (2 oz) grated cheese
50 g (2 oz) onion, roughly chopped
½ teaspoon dried mixed herbs
1 tablespoon shoyu or tamari

1 Sift the flour into a bowl with a pinch of salt. Make a well in the centre, break the egg into it and mix to a paste, then gradually draw in the flour. Mix the milk with the water, then stir into the bowl, but don't over beat. Transfer the batter to a jug, so that it will be easy to pour into the tin, and leave to rest for 30 minutes. This allows the starch to swell, giving a lighter result.

2 Meanwhile, prepare the nut roast: put all the ingredients into a food processor and whiz until you have a smooth mixture that holds together. Form it into 24 cocktail sausages, coat all over with olive oil and place on a baking sheet.

3 Use 2 x 12-hole nonstick mini-muffin tins, each hole measuring 1.5 cm (¾ inch) across and about 1.5 cm (¾ inch) deep. Put ½ teaspoon olive oil into each hole and put the tins into a preheated oven, 220°C (425°F), Gas Mark 7. The oil needs to heat for 10 minutes before you put the batter in.

4 Put the nut roast sausages in the oven at this point (they will take longer to cook than the Yorkshire puddings) and roast for about 15 minutes, or until they are brown and crisp.

5 When the oil in the muffin tins is smoking hot, quickly pour the batter into each hole, filling them about two-thirds full. Bake for 10 minutes, until puffed up and golden. Pop them out of the tin and cool on a wire rack.

6 When you want to serve the Yorkshire puddings, put them on a heatproof serving dish and place a small piece of nut roast on top of each. Put them in the oven, 220°C (425°F), Gas Mark 7, for 4–5 minutes, until hot and puffy. Serve immediately with horseradish sauce.

These are fabulous, and not nearly as much work as you might think because they can be prepared in advance and then just reheated before serving – they'll puff up beautifully.

little broad bean and mint risottos

rice mint wine

serves 24
preparation 30 minutes
cooking 30 minutes

300 g (10 oz) frozen broad beans
1 litre (1¾ pints) vegetable stock
1 tablespoon olive oil
bunch of spring onions, finely chopped
2 garlic cloves, finely chopped
400 g (13 oz) risotto rice
3–4 large sprigs of mint
100 ml (3½ fl oz) dry white wine
50 g (2 oz) butter
100 g (3½ oz) freshly grated Parmesan-style cheese
salt and pepper, to taste
chopped mint, to garnish

1 Cook the broad beans in a little boiling water for 4–5 minutes, then drain and cool them. Pop the bright green beans out of their grey skins and put to one side. Discard the skins.

2 To make the risotto, put the stock into a saucepan and bring to the boil, then reduce the heat and keep the stock hot over a very gentle heat.

3 Heat the olive oil in a large saucepan, add the spring onions and stir, then cover and leave to cook gently for 3–4 minutes, until tender but not browned. Stir in the garlic and cook for a further minute or so.

4 Add the rice to the pan, along with the mint sprigs, and stir over a gentle heat for 2–3 minutes, or until the rice looks translucent, then pour in the wine and stir continuously as it bubbles away.

5 When the wine has disappeared, add a ladleful of the hot stock and stir over a low-to-medium heat until the rice has absorbed the stock. Add another ladleful and continue in this way, adding the broad beans with the final ladleful of stock, until you've used up all the stock, the rice is tender and the consistency creamy. The whole process takes 15–20 minutes.

6 Remove the sprigs of mint, add the butter and half the Parmesan and season with salt and pepper. Immediately transfer the risotto into warmed ramekins, scatter each with a little Parmesan and chopped mint and serve at once, each with a tiny spoon.

Creamy risotto, served piping hot in little ramekins with tiny spoons, makes a sensational party dish and is very easy to do.

jam and cream sponges

jam cream butter

makes 20
preparation 20 minutes
cooking 15–20 minutes

125 g (4 oz) butter, softened
125 g (4 oz) caster sugar
2 eggs
125 g (4 oz) self-raising flour
1 teaspoon baking powder
1 tablespoon water
icing sugar, to dredge

for the filling
3–4 tablespoons raspberry jam
150 ml (¼ pint) double cream, whipped

1 Whisk together the butter, caster sugar, eggs, flour, baking powder and water until light and creamy.

2 Line a 22 x 32 cm (8½ x 12½ inch) Swiss roll tin with nonstick paper and spoon the mixture in, smoothing the surface and making sure the mixture gets into the corners. Bake in a preheated oven, 160°C (325°F), Gas Mark 3, for 15–20 minutes, until risen and firm to a light touch. Remove from the tin and leave to cool on a wire rack.

3 When the cake is completely cold, lay it face down on a board and carefully strip off the paper. Cut the cake into two equal halves and spread one of them with first the jam and then the cream. Press the other half on top, gently but firmly. Use a 3.5 cm (1½ inch) plain round cutter to cut out 20 circles, then put them on to a plate. (They may look neatest upside down – that way if the sponge on top cracks a bit as you cut it, it won't show.)

4 When the cakes are all done, dredge them with icing sugar and keep them in a cool place until required.

These are like darling little Victoria sponge cakes! The discarded 'cuttings' of cake, jam and cream make a great base for a quick trifle, with some fruit, custard and jelly.

pecan and tarragon-stuffed apricots

fruit nuts juice

makes about 26
preparation 15 minutes, plus soaking

250 g (8 oz) ready-to-eat dried apricots
300 ml (½ pint) apple juice
225 g (7½ oz) vegan herb and garlic cream cheese
50 g (2 oz) pecan nuts
small bunch of tarragon

1 Put the apricots into a bowl, cover with the apple juice and leave to soak for 8 hours, or overnight.

2 Drain the apricots and blot with kitchen paper. Stuff each apricot with 1 teaspoon of cream cheese, a pecan nut and a small sprig of tarragon. Arrange them, stuffing-side up, on a serving platter.

This is a delicious treat for your vegan party guests, though everyone will enjoy it. You can get vegan cream cheese at good healthfood shops.

berry skewers with white chocolate dip

fruit cream sauce

makes 20
preparation 15 minutes
cooking 5 minutes

200 g (7 oz) mixed berries, such as strawberries (halved), large blueberries, raspberries, blackberries or baby kiwis (halved)

for the white chocolate dip
100 g (3½ oz) white chocolate, broken into pieces
125 ml (4 fl oz) double cream

1 To make the dip, melt the chocolate in a bowl set over a pan of steaming water. Remove from the heat and stir in the cream. Put into a small serving bowl and set aside to cool.

2 Put one or two berries on each small skewer or cocktail stick – enough for a mouthful. Arrange the skewers around the bowl of white chocolate dip and serve.

With soft fruit, chocolate and cream – you really can't lose, can you?

notes on ingredients

Almond butter Available with no added ingredients such as emulsifiers, from good healthfood shops. There is a brown version and a white one. The oil may separate in the jar – just give it a good stir before use.

Arame seaweed A delicately flavoured seaweed, available dried from good healthfood shops. Simply wash and soak briefly before use.

Bergamot oil An essential oil, a small quantity of which can be used as a flavouring; available from healthfood shops.

Buckwheat Strictly speaking, a seed, though usually classified as a grain. Available from organic food shops, raw or toasted. I prefer to buy raw and, if required, toast it briefly in a dry pan before use.

Caster sugar I like to use Fair Trade golden caster sugar (and other ingredients) when available. Golden caster sugar is not much different in flavour and nutritional content to the white stuff, but I find it more aesthetically pleasing!

Coconut milk Organic coconut milk is much nicer than the non-organic type (which has unnecessary additives) and there's no point in buying the low-fat version as it's just coconut milk with water added – you might as well buy the whole type and add your own water.

Curry leaves Can be found in some large supermarkets and Indian food shops. They freeze well, so it's worth buying up a good supply of fresh ones when you see them – just pop them into the freezer and use when required.

Garam masala A mixture of ground spices added towards the end of cooking to enhance the flavour. Every keen Indian cook has their own recipe, made from spices which they roast, mix and grind themselves, but a shop-bought mixture is fine.

Kaffir lime leaves Can be bought dried, in a jar, from supermarkets; use them up quickly before they lose their magical fragrance.

Ketjap manis A type of soy sauce from Indonesia, which is sweeter and less salty than most other types. It can be found in large supermarkets. Alternatively, you can sweeten ordinary soy sauce with some honey. Store indefinitely in a cool, dry place.

Masa harina A type of cornmeal used to make tortillas. You can buy it at stockists of Mexican food and some large supermarkets.

Mirin A sweet fortified yellow Japanese wine used only for cooking. Found in Asian food stores and some large supermarkets.

Miso Fermented soya paste. Generally speaking, the lighter the miso the milder the flavour and greater the sweetness. Available from healthfood shops and Asian food stores. To get the full health benefits, buy unpasteurized miso and do not boil or overheat it in order to retain its health-giving enzymes.

Nutritional yeast Dried 'inactive' yeast in the form of flakes, available in a tub from upmarket healthfood shops. It has a pleasant cheesy, nutty taste – and is rich in many nutrients.

Palm sugar A brown unrefined sugar used throughout Asia. It is available from large supermarkets and is often sold as a solid block. Soft dark brown muscovado sugar can be substituted.

Pastry From a health and flavour point of view, I prefer pure butter pastry. You can buy it from Dorset Pastry Company, www.dorsetpastry.com, who supply some up-market shops. They make a puff pastry and a shortcrust pastry with cumin seeds, as well as other types. These pastries are unsuitable for vegans, who should use puff pastry made from pure vegetable fat.

Porcini mushrooms in white truffle oil Both truffle oil and porcini and white truffle paste can be found in large supermarkets or Italian food shops.

Ras el hanout A Moroccan spice mixture that you can buy at large supermarkets.

Sesame oil Dark sesame oil can be found in any supermarket and it gives a unique and delectable flavour to Asian dishes. You need only a small amount.

Tahini Like peanut butter, but made from sesame seeds, without additives. I prefer the pale version which is easy to find in supermarkets and healthfood shops. It has a delectable creamy, slightly bitter flavour.

Tamari, shoyu and soy sauce Shoyu is the Japanese word for soy sauce. It is an all-purpose flavouring enhancer; tamari is wheat-free with a stronger flavour. It's important to make sure you buy brands that are traditionally brewed, natural and organic. Available from some big supermarkets and from healthfood shops.

Tamarind A long brown pod with seeds and a tangy pulp used throughout Asia as a souring ingredient. Tamarind paste can be bought in jars in Indian food shops and large supermarkets. Lemon juice may be substituted.

Tofu Tofu is found in the chilled food section of most supermarkets. The type most widely available is 'firm'. I've mostly used this in the recipes because it's a reliable all-purpose type of tofu, suitable for slicing and frying or, with liquid added, for making into a dip or dressing. You can buy other fine, delicate types of tofu in Asian food and organic shops and these are delicious and worth experimenting with if you like tofu.

Toover dhal Also called toor dhal, this is a small golden pulse. It has an earthy, almost smoky flavour and makes a beautiful dhal. Sometimes it's coated in oil to preserve it – wash this off by rinsing it in hot water before cooking. Golden split peas would be the best substitute.

Umeboshi plums/umeboshi paste These have a delicious salty sharpness that enhances many foods. Refrigerated, they will last for ages in their jar. Buy from good healthfood shops.

Unsweetened soya cream Cartons of soya cream equivalent to single cream can be found in healthfood shops and supermarkets in the UK. It does contain a little sugar, but not enough to make it 'sweet' – check the label. In the USA it is not so easy to find substitute unsweetened soya milk, which has a creamy consistency when cooked. A ready-whipped soya cream in an aerosol, and another that you can whip yourself, have recently become available – I find them overly sweet.

Vege-Gel Vegetarian gelatine available from supermarkets. It's easy to use and sets very quickly.

Vegetable stock Marigold vegetable bouillon, a powder which comes in a tub, makes beautiful vegetable stock. Most supermarkets sell it, as do healthfood shops, and there is a vegan version that doesn't contain lactose.

Vegetarian Worcester sauce Can be bought from healthfood shops and some big supermarkets. (The problem with ordinary Worcestershire sauce is that it contains anchovy extract.)

Vinegars While you can get away with just one type of vinegar – I'd choose organic cider vinegar – it's useful to have two or three different ones. Rice vinegar is light and suitable for Chinese and Japanese dishes, while Balsamic has a wonderfully rich, sweet flavour: the more you spend on it, the better it will be.

Wakame seaweed A leafy seaweed, a bit like spinach to look at and with a mild, yummy flavour of the sea. Available dried from good healthfood shops.

Wasabi A strong green Japanese horseradish condiment with a hot mustard taste. It is available as a powder or a paste in large supermarkets and Asian food shops. English mustard can be substituted.

Wild mushrooms Supermarket wild mushroom mixtures can be good value, though for a real treat and a no-expense-spared meal nothing can replace a few precious chanterelles, morels or some fresh porcini. Although they're very expensive, because they weigh very little you get a lot for your money. Dried mushrooms are good value – I especially like dried morels that you can buy at some big supermarkets.

Frying

The healthiest way to deep-fry is to use rapeseed or groundnut oils, which are stable at high temperatures (and therefore healthier), and discard them after use. I use a wok, which has a large surface area so you use less oil or, if I'm doing just a little frying, a small saucepan. For shallow-frying and roasting I generally use olive oil, which is my standard all-purpose oil, but you should refer to the individual recipe.

To grill and skin a red pepper

To grill and skin a red pepper, cut the pepper in half and remove the core, stem and seeds. Place the halves rounded-side up on a grill pan and grill on high for about 10 minutes, or until the skin is blistered and black in places and the flesh tender. Remove from the heat and allow to cool, then peel off the skin.

Toasting hazelnuts

If you're starting with the skinned type (which are the most widely available), either toast them under a hot grill for a few minutes, stirring them after 1–2 minutes so they toast evenly, or put them on a baking tray and roast in a moderate oven –180°C (350°F), Gas Mark 4. They'll take only 8–10 minutes, so watch them carefully and remove them from the hot baking tray immediately they're done so they don't go on browning. To toast unskinned hazelnuts, that is, those still in their brown skins, proceed as described, but they'll take about 20 minutes in the oven. Let them cool, then rub off the brown skins with your fingers or a soft cloth.

Vegan recipes

Many of the recipes in this book are naturally vegan and are labelled as such. A lot more can easily be made vegan by making simple substitutions such as using olive oil or vegan margarine instead of butter, soya instead of dairy cream, maple syrup instead of honey, and vegan puff pastry (read the label) instead of all-butter puff pastry. Here are some suggested vegan alternatives:

Non-vegan	**Vegan**
butter	vegan margarine
milk	soya milk
cream	soya cream
yogurt	soya yogurt
cream cheese	vegan cream cheese
goats' cheese	vegan cream cheese
feta cheese	vegan feta cheese
Cheddar (or other firm) cheese	vegan Cheddar (or other firm) cheese
Parmesan-style cheese (grated)	vegan Parmesan cheese
paneer	firm tofu or firm vegan cheese
mayonnaise	vegan mayonnaise
hollandaise sauce	vegan mayonnaise
honey	maple syrup

menu plans

Barbecue

Green olives with mixed peppercorns, and coriander (V) *(see page 152)*
Spice-crusted tofu with maple glaze (V) *(see page 136)*
Courgette and sweetcorn cakes with chilli sauce (V) *(see page 128)*
Lemon-glazed and seared halloumi with herb salad *(see page 86)*
Buckwheat and mango tabbouleh (V) *(see page 151)*
Sangria fruit salad with almond shortbreads *(see page 116)*

Family meal

Roast potatoes in sea salt and balsamic vinegar (V) *(see page 48)*
Chickpea flatcake topped with lemon- and honey-roasted vegetables *(see page 65)*
Strawberries in rose jelly (V) *(see page 115)*

Garden celebration menu

Bloody Mary jellies *(see page 32)*
Salad of warm artichokes and chanterelles *(see page 15)*
Individual pea, spinach and mint pithiviers *(see page 78)*
Parsnips in sage butter *(see page 46)*
Pink Champagne granita marbled with raspberries (V) *(see page 118)*

Romantic supper

Sesame roasted asparagus with wasabi vinaigrette (V) *(see page 38)*
Brie and cranberry soufflés *(see page 76)*
Melting chocolate puddings *(see page 96)*

Impromptu supper

Crisp tofu with tomato and lemon grass sambal (V) *(see page 37)*
Rice noodles with chilli-ginger vegetables (V) *(see page 56)*
Nectarines roasted with lavender *(see page 114)*

Informal meal

Polenta chip stack with dipping sauces (V) *(see page 40)*
Bubble-and-squeak cakes with beetroot relish *(see page 68)*
White chocolate gelato with citrus drizzle *(see page 121)*

New Year party buffet

Smoked tofu mini-skewers with satay dip (V) *(see page 175)*
Baby Yorkshire puddings with nut roast and horseradish *(see page 176)*
Little broad bean and mint risottos *(see page 178)*
Jam and cream sponges *(see page 180)*
Berry skewers with white chocolate dip *(see page 182)*

Supper for friends

Rosemary sorbet (V) *(see page 26)*
Refritos gateau *(see page 71)*
Fruit fajita pudding *(see page 158)*

Thanksgiving/Festive dinner

Canapés: bruschette with three toppings *(see page 162)*
Tomato and Parmesan tarts with basil cream *(see page 36)*
Carrot, parsnip and chestnut terrine with red wine gravy *(see page 92)*
Cabbage with sesame and ginger (V) *(see page 46)*
Fig tarte tatin with ginger cream *(see page 104)*

Vegan feast

Chilled melon soup with mint granita (V) *(see page 24)*
Portobello steaks en croûte *(see page 84)*
Braised whole baby carrots and fennel (V) *(see page 44)*
Coconut and kaffir lime panna cotta (V) *(see page 112)*

index

N

O

P

R

acknowledgements

Writing a book like this would not be possible without the help and expertise of many people and I would like to thank them all. Firstly, my wonderful editor, Sarah Ford, for having the idea and contributing many wonderful, mouthwatering ideas, and Alison Goff for her enthusiasm and support for the project. I would also like to say a special, big thank you to my daughter Claire who, as luck would have it, was at home while I was writing this book and her taste buds, editing skills and creativity were invaluable. I would like to thank Jason Lowe for the fantastic photographs of the food, and Sunil Vijayakar for cooking the food so beautifully and Mary for helping him so ably; also the editorial team: Jessica Cowie, Barbara Dixon (it was so nice to work with you again, Barbara) and Jo Lethaby. A huge thank you, too, to the art department, especially Tracy Killick and Joanna MacGregor, for producing such a beautiful design and making this book look so attractive. Thanks, too, to my agent, Barbara Levy, and to my dear husband for his unwavering support and help.

Executive Editor Sarah Ford
Senior Editor Jessica Cowie
Executive Art Editor Joanna MacGregor
Design Grade Design Consultants, London
Production Manager Ian Paton

Photography Jason Lowe © Octopus Publishing Group Limited
Food Stylist Sunil Vijayakar
Prop Stylist Rachel Jukes

The Publishers would like to thank Ceramica Blue, 10 Blenheim Crescent, London W11 1NN for the kind loan of some of the props for photography.